Marisol Garc...

M.ª José Medi...

NATIONAL PARKS IN THE CANARY ISLANDS

1st National Award «Everest, 1983»

Translated by: Edward Barreto and
Pilar P. de Valdelomar.

Photographs: Oronoz
Faustino Castilla
Ciganovic
Juan M. Ruiz

EDITORIAL EVEREST, S. A.

MADRID • LEON • BARCELONA • SEVILLA • GRANADA • VALENCIA
ZARAGOZA • BILBAO • LAS PALMAS DE GRAN CANARIA • LA CORUÑA
PALMA DE MALLORCA • ALICANTE — MEXICO • BUENOS AIRES

NATIONAL PARK «CAÑADAS DEL TEIDE»

The Island of Tenerife is g e o m o r p h o l o g i c a l l y characterized by a mountain range that crosses the island from the Northeast to the Southwest. The maximum heights are reached at the «Cirque of the Ravines» —Circo de las Cañadas— where the imposing Teide, 3 717 meters high, emerges like a true titan. This is the highest mountain, not only in the islands but also in the entire country.

The National Park Cañadas del Teide stretches through the municipalities of Guía de Isora, Icod de los Vinos, La Orotava and Santiago del Teide. This park, with more than 130 square kilometers is located on an ancient, huge crater that constitutes an enormous caldera with an average height of 2 100 meters above sea level. There are three geological theories about the creation of this region: explotion, caving in and

The Roques, Cañadas and Teide, the volcano.

4

The landscape at the National Park «Cañadas del Teide» is quite impressive.

erosion; or else, a combination of these three phenomenons. But whatever its genesis was, what is undeniable is that it exists as a most impressive geological monument.

In reality there are two semi-calderas separated by a group of rocky formations known as Roques de García. The western cirque, smaller than the eastern one, shows few physical irregularities. Here there are wide spaces of «malpaís» (rough volcanic terrain) of great beauty: Llano (Plains) of Ucanca and Llano de la Santidad. The eastern cirque is somewhat higher than the western one; its profile is more irregular, with a series of volcanic cones intermixed with numerous lava defiles and gorges that make a multicolored ensemble.

In the South, East and West areas of the Park there are a series of escarpments that

At the Cañadas del Teide Park the geography is exuberant.

surround it. On the bottom of these cliffs are found several ravines that are known as the Cañadas del Teide (Teide Ravines). A ravine is a flat cut in the earth's surface of sedimentary yellowish color where the eroded material from the walls of the caldera is accumulated.

These ravines here were utilized by the «Guanche» n a t i v e s , w h o w e r e transhumant shepherds. From the culture of these ancient inhabitants of the Park we have important vestiges, such as the many archeological findings and the sepulchral sites found so far.

◀ *Mounts of Esperanza. In the background the Teide.*

Seven are the main Ravines, each one having its own name: Ravine of Diego Hernández. Very wide; it has a wide range of colors.

Ravine of Pilas. Its name is derived from the small rock mounds that emerge from the sandy plains, forming a rather odd combination of black and white shapes.

Ravine of the Valley of Piedras Arrancadas (Removed Rocks) with large stone blocks that came from Montaña Rajada (Cracked Mountain).

Ravine of Camellita, with a series of flatlands with scattered hillocks that bring to mind Saharian landscapes, with desert-type dunes.

Hoya del Montón de Trigo

The «malpaís» (barren volcanic land) covers ample areas of the Park.

(Hollow of the Heap of Wheat) is a white, level depression situated between the elevated mounds of volcanic ash and the escarpment walls.

Ravine of Mareta, that gets its name from the fact that when it rains or the thaw arrives, a large pond is formed. The monst beautiful ravine is Llanos de Ucanca (Plains of Ucanca).

Ravine Pedro Méndez, where the recent lava has taken very fancy shapes that have been given names, for instance Zapatilla (Slipper) and Sombrerito (Small Hat).

A few million years after the formation of the concavities of the Ravines, and in recent times in the geological scale, the most impressive range in the island came to existence:

The «Cañadas del Teide» Park can be visited following any of its many interior roads.

The renowned colors of the land in the vicinities of Teide are a must to the visitor.

the gigantic mountains of Teide and Pico Viejo, reaching a height of 1 700 meters on the lowest part of the cirque, and situated near its central area.

The Teide and Pico-Viejo constitute two strata-volcanoes with steep slopes of up to 20°-25°; their gorges form narrow valleys. Pico-Viejo reaches a height of 3 000 m; its deep bowl-shaped crater is 750 meters wide in diameter and 100 meters deep. The crater of Ancient-Teide known as Rambleta of 3 500 m height is occupied by the Pitón volcano, which emerged later and from which black molten lava was ejected and scattered along the steep gradients forming rosette-like lava designs. The

13

Pitón is topped by a small crater that still shows signs of residual activity in the form of sulphuric emanations; the gases come out at a temperature of 80° C.

There is also another series of parasite volcanoes, as well as other of basaltie type.

The last eruption took place in the Eastern slope of the cone. The lava was ejected from the central side of the volcano on the spot known as the Nose of Teide. Its recentness is manifested when observing the paths formed by the lava.

This volcanic cone that emerged from the ancient caldera can be seen, not only from any place in Tenerife, but also from the other islands of the Archipelago when the weather is clear. All the landscape at the foothills and base of the majestic Teide is wholly volcanic. Wide areas of «malpaís» cover with rocks these highlands. Near the National Inn there is an area called «Los Azulejos» (The Tiles), with green blue, red, yellow and black rocks making a true orgy of colors. Nearby, and stretching along two

kilometers, stands the group known as Roques de García, the most spectacular formation seen at the Park Cañadas del Teide. The Roques are huge boulders of different size that stand scattered along the central area of the crater.

The National Park was closed on January 22, 1954, when its total area was 11 866 hectares. The Park was later reclasified and its total area convers today 13 571 hectares. Chronologically it is the third national park in Spain, and the fifth in what regards to its size. It is the largest park in the Canary Islands.

If the National Park is compared with the rest of the island of Tenerife, there are obvious differences, not only in the landscape but also in the weather. The weather in these mountains is affected by four determining factors: their latitude, their oceanic situation, their altitude and their exposure.

Because its average height of more than 2 000 m, and the fact of being protected from the North winds by the elevated

Impressive boulder; one of the «Roques de García».
In the background stands the Teide. ▶

The Plains of Ucanca resemble a sea of petrified lava.

The Teide volcano stands majestically dominating the landscape.

rock walls of the gigantic crater, the Park have a continental subdesertic weather, completely different than the coastal weather.

The sky around here remains deep blue most of the time, and fog is only seen a few days a year. The total of rainfall is quite minimum, averaging between 300 and 400 mm per year, which mainly fall in the winter and therefore falling either as snow or ice.

Winter in the Park causes snow that sometimes covers the top of the mountain, and on occasions it is seen covering the slopes and even the Ravines. It is in this season when a very peculiar phenomenon takes place: the «cencellada», when at dawn some plants and rocks appear covered with thick layers of ice.

At times the highest parts of the volcanic cone cannot be seen, not even from the Cañadas, for halfway on its slopes appears a ring of clouds that hides the summit from sight.

The intense cold at night and

Two views of the Cañadas at the spurs of the volcano.

the strong day heat makes differences in the temperature of many degrees. Finally, another characteristic of the weather conditions seen in this place is the high degree of dryness in the pure air; the level of humidity stands usually under the fifty per cent mark in the months of June and July.

Despite the extreme climatologic conditions of the Park, there is a rich vegetal world, made up of a great variety of species, with a predominance of local endemic species. It is in the Cañadas where the volcanic products are more meteorized and where more micro-climates have been originated that help the most striking species to grow, specially in the spring. It is at this time of the year when a countless variety of multicolored flowers are born from the volcanic residues to adorn the dark ground.

In the Park there are few trees. The cedars of the Canary Islands are seen by the cliffs, almost hanging in the space, and lending their beauty to these barren walls. The pines trees of the Islands grow on the mountain passes and can be seen standing very far apart from one another on the ecarpments of the Cirque. The Radiata pine has been introduced into the Park by man. This is a species of pine not recommended for the park, because being an exotic species it could harm and alter the ecologic balance of the area.

Among the many plants that grow in the Park we can mention: Teide's Broom, which is the most commonly seen herb growing here; it may be seen everywhere, and when it blossoms it gives many white-pinkish flowers with a soft perfume. Another abundant plant is a type of cytisus with yellow flowers and a characteristic resinous smell. The most spectacular plant of the Park is the red Tajinaste, that grows to be 2 meters tall and grows in colonies on the slopes of the Caldera with its vertical stem covered with bright red flowers. Another plant is the blue of spicy Tajinaste, also a very striking species with deep blue flowers.

Worthy of mention among

Daisy of Teide.

all the species of plants growing in the Park are the numerous endemic varieties, for instance the woolly-blue flowered Teide's herb, the lilacpink flowered Teide's stock, the very narrow leafed Pajonera, with deep yellow thorns, Teide's daisy, growing in the highest places of the mountains, the flowered moss, and the «cliff's cake», to mention just a few.

However, the true treasure of the Park consists of two unique species: the Rose of Guanche, dedicated to the memory of the last Guanche native; and the legendary Teide Violet, a flower that grows alone on the fumaroles of the volcano, perfectly camouflaged in the lava crevices.

The fauna life of the Park is rather scarce if it is compared with the Flora life. Among the mammals thriving in the Park are the bush hares, abundant in this area; the Moorish hedgehog, unmistakable by its quills; the wild cat and the common rats and mice found near human quarters.

Three birds of prey are seen in the skies of the National Park: the migratory falcon, in danger of becoming extinct and very seldon seen in the Park; the kestrel, somewhat more abundant, and the sparrow hawk. Among these birds' most common sources of food are the bush hares and wild doves. This latter bird makes its nests on the cliffs of the Caldera and its flight is easily recognized by

Stock flower of Teide.

A beautiful panorama of the National Park «Cañadas del Teide».

«Pajonera» shrub in the Park.

The «Cake of the Cliff».

Easter's Flower.

Bird of Paradise.

the white spot it has on the lower part of its wings. Another prey is the Moorish partridge, that makes its nest on the ground in broom bushes.

Other species of birds found here are the raven, which is seen almost everywhere; the royal shrike, living on the highest places of the mountains and feeds on reptiles; the canary, native to the islands; the titmouse; the common sparro–; the robin, and Teide's chaffinch, whose beautiful blue feathers are remarkable.

The bird in charge of the sanitation duties in the Park is the Egyptian vulture; it feed on the dead bodies of animals, thus getting rid of all the possible sources of infection. The flying patterns of this bird resemble those of the common stork. There are very few of these vultures left in the Park.

A very abundant vertebrate inhabiting these volcanic territories is the stained lizard; its scales are usually dark although the tones vary from animal to animal. The largest ones can be 30 centimeters long. This lizard feeds on plants and insects, both of which are found all over the island. About 400 different species of insects have been classified so far in the Park, many of which are endemic to these latitudes.

On the other hand, visitors can get to the Park from anywhere in the island, for it is located practically in the island's center.

— From the north via Orotava Road to the Cañadas (29 km).

— From the south via Visaflor Road direct to the Cañadas (16 km).

— From the east via the lateral road that borders the island and that starts at the Lagoon (43 km).

— From the west via the Chío-Boca de Tauce Road (14 km). The Orotava-Vilaflor Road crosses the Park from the kilometer 32 up until the kilometer 52 at Boca de Tauce. Besides this asphalt general road there are three additional forestal access roads:

Pico Viejo, on the southern slopes of Teide.

The modern funicular railway at Teide volcano.

«Tajinaste»
in blossom.

— The longest (17 km) starts at the Interpretation Center and leads to the National Tourism Inn. This is the route known as the Route of the Cañadas, bordering the walls of the Caldera along its eastern and southern sections.

— The second road starts at the Orotava-Vilaflor road and goes up the side of Montaña Rajada (Craked Mountain) as far as Montaña Blanca (White Mountain).

— The third road starts at the general road, precisely at the spot opposite the funicular railway; this road passes through the Center of Services of the Park and joins the Route of the Cañadas at Cañada de la Mareta.

In the Park and vicinities there are several buildings where different services to the visitors are offered: The Interpretation and Reception Center for Tourists. This building is perfectly adapted to its surrounding area; it has a small solar energy plant to satisfy its requirements. This is a building worth visiting, for in 20 minutes the visitor obtains important information about the Park and can also watch a very interesting film.

In the area of Portillo, outside the Park limits, there is a series of restaurants and souvenir stores frequently visited by tourists.

The Tourist National Inn of Cañada Blanca has 52 beds and diverse leisure facilities. Here at the Cañada Blanca and on nearby Roques de García there is a rest area provided with a variety of services to the visitors.

The funicular railway, along the southern slope of the Teide goes from Blanquiales (2 356 m) to Rambleta (3 555 m) in an ascension that takes 8 minutes. The funicular works from sunrise to 4 p.m.

The Refuge of Altavista at Rambleta (3 250 meters). This inn has 40 beds, electricity, a bar and kitchen. In order for visitors to stay at this place

overnight it is necessary for them to obtain a permit at the Island Tourist Board in Santa Cruz de Tenerife.

Following are some recommendations for visitors to this National Park:

Same can be visited throughout the year, but it is truly splendorous in May and June, when all the plants bloom.

The climb to the top of Teide takes about 25 minutes walking from the funicular terminal station; in the winter the snow makes the ascent more difficult. In any case, adequate shoes must be worn for the trek.

To climb the Teide without using the funicular it is possible to take a path that starts at Montaña Rajada and goes up to the top. When walking in the Park the visitors must follow the existing, signalled paths, for it is difficult to walk on the solidified lava.

It is forbidden to take home volcanic souvenirs and to cut plants in the Park.

The best hours to visit the

The National Tourist Inn at «Cañadas del Teide» stands on the base of Guajara mountain.

top of the volcano are at sunset and specially at sunrise. An unforgettable experience is to watch the shadow of the mountain over the island of Gomera and see how it decreases in size in no time. Another interesting sight is to watch the twilight phenomenon at 4 000 meters high in the midst of a landscape where the natural forces are manifested at their highest degree of intensity and drama. To be able to watch these two natural shows it is adviced to go to Altavista to behold the sunset from there, spend the night at the inn, and in the morning, before sunrise, walk to the top to participate in the beginning of the new day.

In order to know the Park in detail the following itinerary is recommended: On leaving Santa Cruz de Tenerife and past the Lagoon, take the dorsal road of the island. The first stop can be made at the lookout of Ortuño, from where hundreds of acres of picturesque pine forests can be seen, having the Teide as backdrop. Farther up is the Mirador of Cumbres (Heights Mirador), offering a view of over a third of the island. The same road goes straight to Portillo de la Villa, where the Center of Interpretation can be visited.

As soon as the access checkout point for this forestal road is crossed one is in the Seven Cañadas, having left behind the Mountain of Black Sands to the left side. Next comes Cañada of Diego Hernández, one of the most important ravines from the floral point of view. To the left stands Montaña Colorada (Red Mountain) with its Chiqueras Peak (2 365 m). To the right lies the Valley of Trujillo. When this Cañada is crossed, one encounters a «guanche» (natives original to the island) refuge located on the wall of the Caldera. This refuge is known as the Cave of Diego Hernández.

After Risco Verde (Green Cliff) and always following the road on the base of the cliff wall, the visitor arrives at Cañada de las Pilas (Ravine of the fountains) followed by Cañada de la Angostura (Narrow Ravine) and Cañada

«Boca de Tauce», one of the two natural entrances to the Cañadas park.

de la Grieta (Ravine of the Crevice), where there is a natural fountain. Then comes the small Cañada of Camellita (Ravine of the small Camel), which is also very interesting for its plants. When the Roque de la Grieta is passed and left behind to the left, one enters Cañada del Montón de Trigo (Ravine of the Heap of Wheat). To the left of this ravine is seen

«Plains of Ucanaca» in the Cañadas, completely covered with lava.

the Degollada de Guajara and further ahead stands Guajara Mountain (2 715 m). It is at the higher places of this mountain where the Violet of Teide grows. The Cañada that comes next is Mareta where the route of the Cañadas joins the forestal pathway that comes from the Center of Services of the Park. Then comes Cañada del Capricho (Fancy Ravine). Going ahead along the base of Guajara Mountain, crossing another access control point and leaving behind Montaña de Piedra (Stone Mountain), 2 226 m, one arrives at the general main road, near the Inn. Here one must go the opposite direction towards Vilaflor. On the right, next to Roques de García is the area of Azulejos (Tiles).

This road goes through the Plains of Ucanca, bordering Cañada of Pedro Méndez on its left side, and goes up to the westernmost wall of the National Park, the Plain of Santidad. From here one has a great view of the Mountain of Chahorra or Pico Viejo (Old Peak).

The same road is taken on the way back as far as the National Inn. It is worth to walk to the Mirador of Ucanca that offers a view of the entire western area of the National Park.

On the way to the Interpretation Center, after passing Cañada Blanca, one must take the road that goes to the funicular station. Here the funicular can be taken and from the place it stops one can walk up to the top. After visiting the summit and having gone down on the funicular, the general road can be taken again. It goes along the road known as Vueltas del Carnero (Curves of the Ram). On the left hand side of this road there is an exit to a forestal road that goes first to Montaña Rajada and then, after an ascent of sharp turns, to Montaña Blanca. Here there is an impressive panorama of the entire east and south areas of the Cirque of the Cañadas.

The same road is taken on the way back to start the last stage of the tour of the Park; this last lap takes the whole day. The road borders on the right the Valley of Removed

«The Shoe of the Queen», a singular geological formation at the Plains of Ucanca.

A sea of clouds floating over Orotava Valley.

Rocks, Montaña de los Pinos (Mountain of Pines), and Montaña Mostaza (Mustard Mountain). Thus one arrives at the Center of Interpretation and Portillo de la Villa.

To return to the city of Santa Cruz de Tenerife the north road can be taken until Orotava, and from there go to Puerto de la Cruz.

In the island of Tenerife, besides the National Park, there are other places of great natural interest, such as the Region of Anaga, in the far north end of the island, a very rough region with remains of laurisilvas. The Region of Teno, on the far eastern end of the island; this region is based on an awesome rocky eminence with huge cliffs and laurisilva tree remains on its walls. The Barranco del Infierno (Hell's Gorge) is spectacular and has a lot of botanical and zoological endemic species.

NATIONAL PARK
OF CALDERA
DE TABURIENTE

The island of San Miguel de la Palma, with a total area of 728 square kilometers, is located in the northwestern far end of the Archipelago of the Canary Islands. As the other «Islas Afortunadas» (Lucky Isles), this one is of volcanic origin, but differs from the others by its vast supply of fresh water sources, both underground and on the surface of the island.

The central area of the island is occupied by the impressive geological formation of Caldera de Taburiente, with a maximum axis of 7 kilometers and whose summit is the highest place in the island, Roque de los Muchachos (Peak of the Boys), 2 423 meters above sea level. It was thus called because when it is watched from a distance the top looks like a group of children. From the top one can see, not only the entire island of La Palma, but also Isla Verde,

The Hermitage and the Pine Tree of the Virgin, spurs of the «Cumbrecita» in the limits of Caldera de Taburiente.

Bright paths of vegetation descend to the interior of the caldera.

and the islands of Gomera, Hierro, Tenerife and Gran Canaria. It is only possible to enter Caldera de Taburiente (Taburiente Cauldron) through foothpaths and bridle paths. Several fountains are born here; when their waters join they form an abundant stream known as Taburiente River.

Besides the peak of Roque de los Muchachos, there are several others of important height: La Cumbrecita; El Corralejo, 2 044 m; El Cedro, 2 206 m; Piedra Llana, 2 317 m; La Cruz, 2 350 m, and Roque Palmero, 2 352 m.

This privileged Park was one of the twelve cantons or Guanche kingdoms in which the island of Palma was divided. The kingdoms of Aceró, as this natural impregnable fortress was

The bottom of the Caldera appears surprisingly crossed by several streams.

called, was governed by a Mencey (native chief). When on September 29, 1491 Alfonso Fernández de Lugo arrived at the island, he rapidly conquered all the cantons, with the exception of the one of Aceró, in those times ruled by Mencey Tanansú. The efforts of the Castillian to penetrate the Caldera through its only natural entrance, Barranco de las Angustias (Cliff of Anguish) were useless, for the Guanche natives controlled all the movements of their enemies from strategical positions on the walls of the cliff.

The Spanish Captain-General, using a stratagem, arranged for a negotiation meeting with the chief in Aridane, outside the Caldera. Tanansú, naively accepted the proposal, and when he had left his refuge he fell into the trap, and after a long boody battle he was captured on May 3, 1492. This is the story of how this historical place, also a religious place for the Guanches, was conquered by the Spanish corwn.

From 1557 until present days, the Caldera de Taburiente is property of the Community or County Estate of the Farms of Argual and Tazacorte. At present there are more than 1 600 joint owners. It must be pointed out that the title of property is not determined by a given number of acres, but by the hours, minutes and seconds of water it gets.

The peaks that encircle the Park are seen through the vegetation.

When the Caldera de Taburiente was created on October 6, 1954, it had a surface of 3 500 hectares, and was the 4th National Park in Spain. When it was later reclassified, its size was increased to 4 690 hectares. It is now the seventh National Park in what regards to its size.

The Caldera de Taburiente is, as its name indicates, a large depression whose bottom is about 600-900 meters above sea level: on the other hand, the peaks that make up the rocky circle that surround the Park sometimes surpass the 2 400 meters. It was probably originated as a huge explosion crater many kilometers in diameter. The abundance and strength of the ditches are the vestiges of a very intense eruptive activity. The most powerful emissions came from

The vegetation is varied in the Park.

The drastic drops in the mountains range between 800 and 2 423 meters.

here and formed the insular building, shaping it into its original figuration.

It resembles a horseshoe opened to the southeast on the deep Gorge of Angustias, which is the outlet for all the waters. The total diameter of the Caldera is 10 kilometers; it has a surface drop of up to 1 500 meters between Roque de los Muchachos and the bottom. The escarpments —the first one of which is 750 m high— are grooved with gorges, crevices and buttes that at the bottom are oddly combined. Many ditches have resulted to be in an upright position.

The Caldera is extremely intricate inside. There are

49

A view of the bottom of the Caldera.

gorges and large boulders everywhere, some coming from the slopes and others created in situ. From the very few access pathways into the Park, the most commonly utilized are the ones that go through the Terrace of Tenerra, at the base of Time Mountain; and the path that follows part of the drainage ditch. There is a third access road via La Cumbrecita, but it is the most dangerous one.

The effects of erosion have caused a series of ridges that can be seen surprisingly balanced in the escarpments. The mass of rocks, with different layers of materials, mirrors diverse, changing tones when it is struck by the sunbeams: purples and oranges in the afternoons; greys and ghost-like hues when the clouds touch the base of the peaks.

The final stretches of the

Roque Idafe in the background, as seen through the local vegetation.

Cliff of Anguish go through a mass of sedimentary elements (the most important in the Archipelago) of alluvial origin, that shows the existence of different marine levels in the history of the island.

On the divisory lines of the small torrential valleys there are several rocks of monolithic aspect, some of which, for instance the one known as Idafe, were used by the natives to worship their god Abora, and had an important role in the religious life of the Guanches.

Erosion continues its implacable action, widening and carving the hollows of the slopes of the Caldera. This erosion becomes more obvious in the raining season, when the waters that leave the Park carry with them a lot of materials in suspension.

The limits between the basal group and the layers of basalt

51

Two overwhelming views of Caldera de Taburiente.

constitute an important aquiferous supply. Water is one of the most important natural, beautiful elements in this volcanic landscape. Many fountains that spring from the earth join their waters to form brooks and waterfalls in the most exotic corners. Inside the Caldera the noise of the flowing or falling water from the high cliffs is another attraction of this marvelous natural scenery.

The Falls of Desfondada is with its 150 meters drop one of these many amazing sights. Most of the fountains and springs in this Park have clear, fresh water, but there are others that come from Barranco de Almendro Amargo (Cliff of the Sour Almond Tree) whose waters have a high content of ferric materials. These waters are yellowish-reddish, and stain with this color the riverbeds and banks.

In the Caldera there are two main hydrological riverbeds,

Taburiente and Almendro Amargo. Both meet at the place of Dos Aguas, very near the Park limits, but on the outside; Dos Aguas is where Barranco de las Angustias starts. It is also here where all the waters of the Caldera have their only natural outlet.

At Dos Aguas the waters that come from the Park are channelled and taken to cultivation land. The sharp drops in the level of the surface of up to 2 000 m that occur at the Caldera are the cause for a very drastic climatic contrast between the top and bottom regions of the ridges.

The average rainfall in the Park ranges between 900-1 000 mm per year. In the winter this rain becomes snow at the highest places of the mountains. A very common phenomenon is the development of large masses of clouds that are seen floating inside the Caldera owing to the rising hot air. These clouds disappear at night and return with the new day.

Banana plantation at the Cliff of Angustias; this is a natural outlet place for the waters of the Caldera.

54

Another impressive view from inside the Taburiente.

The plants that grow in the Park are exuberant and large. The Canarian pine is the species most predominantly found here, and the green forests that cover it consist of almost exclusively this pine. It is a tall, pyramid-like tree, whose oldest specimens reach over 60 meters, with a diameter of 3 m at the base of the trunk. Its powerful, radical system and its marked xerophilous characteristics make it the ideal tree for the colonization of volcanic territories. Its abundant branching springs from the trunk in regular verticillates, a feature that makes it different from the other species found in Spain.

The ecological, protector role of this tree on the volcanic soil of the islands has been and will be of extreme importance. On the steep slopes of the National Park the forestal shield created by the Canarian pines is an irreplaceable, and the only natural defense against an accelerated erosion that continuously atracks the walls of the park. This pine is also a tree with a very high fire resistant wood, being able to resprout after forestal fires.

The amagante is another species of vegetal life found growing near the Canarian pines. This type of rockrose, endemic to the Canary Islands, is markedly xerophilous and very frugal; for this reason it can grow on very poor soil. This fact, plus the additional advantage of its easily germinated seeds, make it into a plant specially suited for growing on nearly barren soil, which together with the Canarian pine, has thrived here.

There are other varieties of rockroses growing here which in turn serve to welcome an almost subterraneous parasite, yellow and reddish, the «Batallita» (Small Battle), also known as «Vaquita» (Little Cow), in the other islands.

Inside the Park one can also find varieties of heath and heather. They are known as the «green mountain» in the Canary Islands. The ecological importance of these plants is enormous, for they are not only the source of an abundant organic fertilizer, but their active condensing action on the

«Roque de los Muchachos» (Peak of the Boys), 2 423 m, in the Caldera de Taburiente. This is the highest mountain in the island of Palma. ▶

«Acebiño» tree (Holly).

fog, helps to greatly increase the volume of running water collected on the land on which they grow.

The Canarian beech variety easily reaches the eight meters. Its only growth requirement is to have a humid environment and to be sheltered from the cold. Mixed with the beech grown abundant white flowers that lend their aroma to the air around them. As heather has a higher ecological valence than beech, it can grow farther up in the mountain, leaving the beech and mixing with the pine trees.

In the cliffs, where the humidity is greater, there still are remains of forests of Lauraceaus. There are hollies interwoven with the beech and heather. These trees can grow 12 meters high, and their main features are a smooth trunk with a whitish bark, and branches without leaves; these however, produce white-corollaed flowers late in the spring. Besides the holly trees there are also laurel trees, sometimes known as «loros» (Spanish onomatopoeic for laurel). These trees, some of which can be 12 meters high, grow next to another type of laurel trees, the Apollonia canariense, that chooses the most rugged areas to grow. Their trunks are thick and the flowers hermaphrodite, releasing a mild, characteristic smell. One can also see the «viñatigos» with their straight trunks on the lower end, and abundant branching on the higher part, and the «marmolanes», to mention just a few.

Numerous species of dense plants adapted to rupicolous life on boulders and craggy walls grow everywhere in this National Park. Many of them are endemic to the Islands, for instance the «bejeques», with their large rosettes of carnose leaves that emerge from the drevices in the highest cliffs and it is only after many years of life that blossom with attractive inflorescences; the «Tabaibas», woody plants of brief foliation and in whose stems a lot of water is deposited; the «Verodes» with light green pulpy stalks and articulated branches, to mention just a few of these plants.

The Canarian willow is another species that is often seen growing on the banks of brooks and streams. The lush landscape is further enhanced by several species of «Taginastes». The common fern is the most abundant type of these plants, almost all of them growing in this area.

From the 2 000 meters upwards, where the Canarian pine no longer grows, another endemic plants takes its place: the cytisus. It can be said that owing to lack of competition from other plants, this species is the one that has taken over at these heights. However, even from the 1 700 meters one can see scattered specimens of cytisus in the undergrowth, and as one goes higher along the steep slopes of the Caldera, these plants become more and more abundant until all one can see is forests of this leguminous. **When they flower the air is impregnated with a strong, syrupy aroma.**

In the highest places of these

rugged walls stand like royal crowns, the ancient and weather worn Canarian cedars. This cedar is a geographic variety of the cedar growing in the Peninsula. The Canarian cedars grow showing their twisted trunk and branches almost hanging in the air, and their unmistakable silhouettes are spectacularly contrasted against the blue background.

Also at the summit of the mountains of this National Park grow several endemic physuricole species; among them there is one in danger of becoming extinct. It is the Pansy of the heights that grows in the rocky crevices from which its long hanging branches come out, covered with beautiful blue flowers. The blue Tajinaste and the Broom, from the same family of the cytisus, grow at these altitudes.

Man, who has lived at the Caldera for many years now, although fortunately not in large groups, has cultivated in the places where the slopes are not very steep, cereals, grapes, tobacco and fruits; from these

the gigantic, ancient fig trees are worth mentioning.

The land that has been modified by man has suffered the invasion of a series of introduced species, for instance the «haragán» from México, and the «tedera», used as food for livestock.

The Caldera is also the home of a few vertebrate animals. A few years ago it was still possible to see a small goat with long, straight horns that rolled up as the animal grew older. The female goat had a small udder, and both sexes had a white mound between the fur and skin that made them water resistant. The origin of the goat was unknown, and today this species is extinct owing to multiple interbreeding and relentless hunting for their appetizing fibrous meat.

Some years ago a few moufflons were let free in the Caldera, just as it was done at the National Park of Teide. They did not thrive at the Caldera, but abandoned it and are now considered as animals lost in the Park. For this reason the only mammals living in the Caldera in their wild state are a

Cytisus tree.

few rabbits and some wild cats.

Birds are the vertebrates with the largest number of species here. The sparrow hawk is the only bird of prey seen flying in the Caldera. The wild dove and the laurel dove also thrive in the Park. The endemic crow, the black raven and the singing blackbird are some of the Paseriformes living here. Among the smaller species there is the abundant blue titmouse and the crested whitethroat, here known as «capirote» (Hood) that makes its nests on the bushes.

Among the reptiles, the stained lizard, which is also found at the National Park Teide, lives in the rocky areas of the Caldera. A species of gecko lizard, or tarente, lives in the same area. There is a small type of frogs from the amphibious family.

In order to better enjoy the diverse contrasts of the Caldera of Taburiente, the visitor can go to La Palma by air or by sea on a ferryboat taken in Tenerife. There are three different itineraries to the Park. The first one starts at the town of El Paso, where an asphalted road goes up to the mirador of La Cumbrecita (The little summit). This route is 9 kilometers long. Here there are two additional lookout points, Las Chozas and Roques, offering an imposing view of the Park. The second itinerary starts at Llanos de Andance (Plains of Andance) and can only be covered by jeep or a similarly equipped vehicle for rugged terrain. A winding dirt road takes the visitor to Lomo de los Caballos (Horse Back), followed by Cliff of Anguish and finally by the ascent to La Farola, near the limits of the Park. From there one must continue on foot through a bridle path to enter the Caldera, past the only two houses that exist in the Park: the houses of Tenerra and Taburiente. The third itinerary can be taken to avoid the northern peaks of the Park.

The forestal road starts at the group of houses of Mirca, to the north of Santa Cruz de la Palma; it goes up alon the eastern slopes of the island to Los Andenes (33 km) and from there it continues until it reaches Roque de los Muchachos (36 km), the highest place in the Park and the island.

There are other interesting places in the island: Teneguía Volcano, near Fuencaliente, the southernmost town in the island. This is the last Spanish volcano in activity. The Cave of Belmaco, in Mazo, with its walls having prehistoric inscriptions. The Forest of Tilos, in San Andrés and Sauces; the forest is quite luxuriant and its ferns are enormous.

While in the Park, the visitor can also go to Roque del Idafe, the Fall of Desfondada (distant one hour from Taburiente), and the Cave of Tanausú; the entrance to the cave is under a rock shaped like a human head. The cave is halfway between Tenerra and the group of houses of Taburiente, above the fountain of Fayal.

NATIONAL PARK OF GARAJONAY

The Island of Gomera, with a total area of 380 km, and almost circular in shape, is quite different from the other islands. As in this island there were not any volcanic eruptions in the Quaternary that renovated its natural features, its surface is eroded everywhere; for this reason the island is known as the Island of Cliffs.

In the central area of the island there is a small, flat plateau from which spring in radial form several furrowed cliffs carved in the ground. The National Park takes this entire central plateau as well as the beginning of several ravines. The nearly 4 000 hectares of the Park constitute more than 10 % of the total area of the island. The general outline of the Park is even, consisting of a blend of gorges, hills, slopes and cliffs. Their heights range between 800 m and 1 400 m.

A view of the nearby island of Tenerife with the unmistakable outline of Teide, as seen from the Park of Garajonay.

The ceiling of the Park and the island is the Peak of Garajonay, 1 487 m, which has given its name to the Park.

Over half of the surface of the Park consists of forests created almost exclusively for the protection of the Canarian laurisilva (an endemic family of trees).

The Park, with its 3 974 hectares, will be the ninth chronological Park among the Spanish National Parks. Its creation project is at present being studied at the Congress for its approval. For its size it is the eighth park, being the smallest one in the Canary Islands.

The undulated landscape of the Park is characterized by forests whose splendour is based on the tree that makes it have an homogeneous profile: the laurisilva. The scenery is complemented by the fog, appearing throughout the year, and a most important element, for it contributes to create the unique ecological conditions that make this an exceptional water reservoir.

The forestal uniformity is only interrupted by the peaks or «roques» and the escarpments that are seen on the bound aries of the Park. The peaks are ancient volcanic chimneys through which came out a pasty lave much more acid in composition than the basalt emissions. The «roques» are seen on several places in the island, but acquire their highest expression in the southeastern limit of the park at the area known as Zone of Roques. In a reduced area stand impressively four volcanic domes with the names of Ojilla, Zarcita, La Mula and Ogando, the last mentioned being the most imposing one. Another commanding peak is Cherilepí, in the central area of the Park.

Water is another important element in the Park of Garajonay. There are several permanent fountains in the area of the Park; the most important course of water is the Brook of Cedro, in the zone of the same name and within territories of the Mount of Hermigua. Other important streams are those of Ojilla, in the valley of San Sebastián, Fuensanta and Aguas de los

The dense forests of «laurisilva» trees are the main feature of this island. ▶

Llanos (Waters of the Plains) in Mount Hueco de Agulo, and those of Vallehermoso in Mount Gelina and Chipude.

The weather of the island is determined by the trade winds. These winds cause the sea of clouds that is seen floating above the central plateau and definitively help to create the specific ecological features of the island. The prevalent temperatures are very mild. The average rainfall varies considerably from year to year, ranging between 600 and 800 mm per year. The volume of water is increased owing to the laurisilva trees that condensate the fog and so help to almost double the supply of water. The weather differences between the north and south areas of the Park are minimal; in the north the cliffs are more humid and the laurisilva trees grow more exuberantly.

The Garajonay is basically a botanical Park; the main reason for its creation was to

As seen in these photographs, the vegetation life in the Park of Garajonay is abundant.

protect the exceptional vegetation that grows in it, specially the dense laurisilva forests. The laurisilva tree from the Tertiary was a subtropical species that during the Pliocene was also seen on the Mediterranean river valleys. Today the laurisilva is an endemic tree whose most representative specimens are found in this Park, specially at the Bosque de las Mesetas (Forest of the Plateaus).

Approximately 2 500 hectares from the total surface of the Park are forests. These forests consist of laurisilva, heather-climax and heath-heather.

The laurisilva has different species and its floristic composition varies according to the area where it grows and

Panoramic view of the Forest of Cedro in Garajonay. ▶

to several additional factors.

The most important feature of the laurisilva is its arboreal stratum; it is made up of the following species: Laurel, seen almost everywhere in the Park; «Viñatigo», a tree that grows on the cliffs; Linden, another Canarian endemic variety that grows on the bottom of the valleys; its number in the park is very small. The «acebiño» is another very common species with its red, ripe fruits; «Barbusano» (Apollonias canariense), growing on the scarpments and craggy regions on shady places of the slopes; «Palo Blanco» (White Wood), growing next to the barbusanos; Heath is another important shrub that grows in the laurisilva forests; Heather, perhaps the most common shrub in the island, and Madrone, growing in colonies, producing edible fruits... to mention a few.

The lush, evergreen laurisilva forest and its fog resemble a true forests taken out of afairy tale book. A remarkable peculiarity is the fast decomposition of the vegetation owing to the high degree of humidity that reigns inside the forest.

The shrubbery stratum is represented by a wide regeneration of the arboreal species accompanied by a series of varieties that vary from one area to another and from which the most important are the following: «Follao», an endemic Canarian variety that grows on the bottom and slopes of the gorges; «Verdonasco» or female «follao», growing in the same places; the «Peralillo» or «Peralito» (Pear shrub) another Canarian endemic variety; the «Capitana» or «Alcanutillo», and the pennyroyal, among others.

Many trees appear covered with moss and lichens, and the highly humid outer layer of the soil is a carpet of a great assortment of ferns, among which are the «Penco», growing on the slopes and bottom areas of the gorges; the Black scale fern, abundant in the higher zones; the «pirgua», whose shoots can reach 3 meters long, and the bogs of ferns, the most common variety.

There are also many

The evergreen forest combined with the fog cause an almost unreal landscape. ▶

Heather.

climbing plants and vines, for instance the common ivy; the «Gibalbera», «Norza» and the thornless sarsaparilla.

Plants growing on the ground are not abundant, and the ones that do are definitively umbrageous. From the varieties that are developed in the laurisilva forest we can mention here the «Vileta oviola», wild borage, the large nettle, the forget-me-not or blue shrub, as well as diverse species of geraniaceous.

Heather-climax grows in several areas of the Park, for instance in the south region at Altos de Chorros de Espina, near the peaks of Ojilla, and at Zarcita, in the crags of Cherilepí. The twisted trunks and branches of these ghost-like heathers give the forest a phantasmagoric air; the eerie atmosphere is

Heath-Heather growth.

increased by the frequent fog. The trunks and branches of the trees in this forest are usually covered with moss and lichens. The soil of this heather-climax growth is covered with dense pads of moss and phanerogamous mixed with numerous ferns.

Finally, in the southwest limit of the Park there is a wide area where the heath-heather species prevails.

The tree-like heath-heather shrubs are mingled in capricious patterns over other shrubs. On the soil, together with the moss and lichensm the cytisus and ferns form a green lush carpet.

Also worthy of mention is the area of the Roques. These cliffs are not forested. There is, however, a unique type of plants with many endemic species that grow together with

77

«Viñatigo» plant.

Laurel.

the occasional savin, cedar and madrone trees.

The vertebrate fauna of the Park cannot be considered as rich. Rabbits, introduced by the Spanish conquerors still thrive in the island, and specially in the south of the Park where most of them live. There are also a few Moorish hedgehogs.

A very harmful animal for the «viñatigo» trees is the black rat, not native to the island and without any natural enemies.

The laurisilva forests in the Island of Gomera are the natural habitat for many different Canarian types of birds. Many are the paseriformes that make their moss nests in the laurisilva

79

Forest of «Laurisilva» trees.

Detail of the Forest of Cedro.

trees, especially on the higher forks of the branchs. Among other species are the common chaffinch, the blue titmouse, the kinglet, the robin, several species of whitethroats, and above all, the most abundant bird, the blackbird.

Two Canarian endemic varieties of wild pigeons have lived in these forests since time immemorial: the «Turcón», that makes its nests in the highest trees, and the «rabiche cock pigeon», less abundant and nesting on rocky places.

In the most humid areas of the Park thrives the woodcock or woodcock partridge. There are three birds of prey in the Park; two of them are diurnal, the kestrel and the small eagle, and one is nocturnal, the small owl. Finally, the stained lizard is found living in the most thermophile areas of the Park, especially in the southern slopes.

Plants are seen growing throughout the entire Park of Garajonay.

Contrary to what happens with vertebrate animals, the invertebrate fauna is quite important in the laurisilva forests, with a wide number of endemic species.

As in the island of Gomera there is not an airport, the only possible way to get to the island is by the ferryboat that goes from Los Cristianos in Tenerife to San Sebastián in Gomera. From San Sebastián there is a road to the Park, and in it there are some pathways.

With the exception of a very small National Inn and a few lodging places, it may be difficult to find a place to sleep in the island. However, if the first ferryboat is taken in the morning, and the last one is taken back to Tenerife, the Park can be satisfactorily visited. A recommendation to visitors is that they must wear appropriate clothes and shoes owing to the high degree of

The «roques» (peaks) are an everpresent element of the heights of the Park.

The Forest of Cedro, water and vegetation.

humidity that prevails on the island.

Besides the Park, in the island there are other places of great landscapist beauty, for instance any of the countless gorges that are found throughout the island, and especially in the area of Los Órganos. This is a cliff whose walls stands 100 meters on the Atlantic Ocean. The cliffs and gorges are of volcanic origin, and the pipelike columns resemble an organ. The cliffs are better seen from the ocean.

*There are remarkable natural sights to be admired ▶
in the island of Gomera.*

NATIONAL PARK OF TIMANFAYA

Lanzarote is the nearest of the Canary Islands to the African continent. It is 795 square kilometers and for its size is the fourth island of the Archipelago. The island of Lanzarote received its name from Lancelotto Malocello, a Genoese sailor.

The elongated island, known as the «Island of the Volcanoes» is wholly volcanic, like the other islands of the Archipelago.

Lanzarote is the tragic palaestra for a century-long challenge: on the one hand, the mighty power of natural forces, and on the other hand, man's creative capacity in his struggle for survival. This is perhaps one of the places where this struggle of man against nature has taken the most original aspect. Here one finds one of the most impressive regions of the Canary Islands, the Montañas del Fuego (Mountains of Fire), or

Landscape at the National Park of Timanfaya.

Lava path at Montaña del Fuego (Fire Mountain).

Timanfaya, as they were known in the past.

As one approaches these mountains and the rounded outline of the ridges can be distinguished, one is somehow reminded of something ancient; however, almost all these elevations belong to a group of volcanoes that were developed during the long and impressive eruption of

◀ *A panoramic view of the region of Timanfaya where there were violent volcanic eruptions between 1730 and 1736 and in 1824.*

Timanfaya that lasted for six years, from 1730 to 1736, almost uninterruptedly. Throughout this time the central-western area of the island shook and trembled, the very entrails of the island were cracked and Dantesque tongues of fire emerged through the crevices. The center of the volcanic activity was at the group of mountains of Fuego or Timanfaya, and area five kilometers from east to west and six kilometers wide from north to south. In this

A volcanic prairie at Montañas de Fuego.

Traces of the volcanic eruptions constitute the landscape at Timanfaya.

reduced area over 25 craters were opened that laid waste almost 20 000 hectares with lava, gases, ashes, bombs and lapilli, transforming the ancient, rich valleys of Timanfaya and Miradores into a black, ravaged and totally barren territory.

This central region was the richest in the island, having a group of cultivated valleys where life was lived peacefully in the few villages that disappeared under the layers of lava; all their inhabitants were forced to emigrate.

The six years of intense volcanic activity were followed by a period of tranquility and imperturbation that was interrupted in 1824 by an eruption that lasted from July 31 until October 25, with short periods of calm between these two dates. Although these eruptions were not as severe as the ones in the last century, three new volcanoes emerged. One of the newly created

The geography of Timanfaya is made up of countless volcanic craters, almost connected with the sea.

craters, the one of the Tinguatón volcano, started to emit huge volumes of salted water in liquid and steam, most progably coming from an underground stream connected with the sea.

These historical eruptions turned the geography of the island into a landscape very

levelling outlines, meteorizing the ground, and allowing the vegetation to grow and colonize this volcanic land.

The total area occupied in the island by the volcanos and fields of lava originated as the result of said eruptions comprises 200 square kilometers. This can give us an idea of the magnitude of the phenomenons and it also means that the enormous extent of lava fields or «malpaís» (barren volcanic land and name given to this territory by the islanders) and the volcanic cones in the area of the Mountains of Fire, is only a small fraction of the fields with historical volcanoes existing in the island.

On August 9, 1974 was promulgated the creation of the 8th Spanish National Park. In its reclassification the Park was given the same area it had when it was first created: 5 107 hectares, which places it in the sixth position among the Spanish National Parks in regards to size.

The National Park is situated within the municipalities of Yaiza and Tinajo, precisely where volcanic activity has been more

different from the one seen on the other Canary Islands. In the other islands the many years without volcanic activity have left their indelible print,

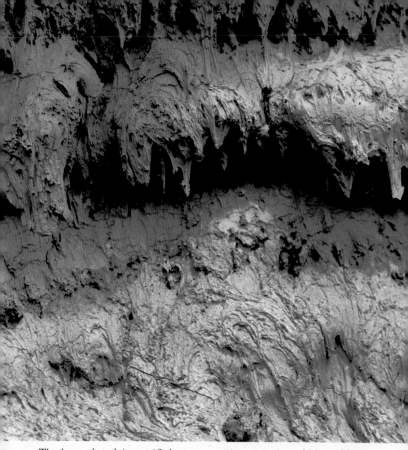

The lava, shaped in petrified waves, acquires an eerie outlook at Montañas del Fuego.

intense. In its eastern limits it borders with the Atlantic Ocean. The Park is 5 107 hectares and has an approximate outside perimeter of 30 kilometers. Almost all the area is property of the local Town Hall; this allows direct action to be taken by the Insular Council of Lanzarote.

The mineral world is the natural realm with the widest representation in this Park. Here all sorts of geological phenomenons can be seen, mainly those of volcanic origin and those resulting from the powerful, inner forces inside the earth's crust.

The paths made by the lava are unmistakable, for they appear like sharp tracts descending from the volcanic cones, solidified on the primitive soil, scoriform in shape, forming large masses of broken rocks, and constituting the main ingredient for the typical geography of these lava fields. Here the landscape is harsh, monochromatic, tormented, rugged and aggressive, but at the same time it is beautiful in its immense loneliness and undescribable for the strength of inanimate matter.

Looking around one can discover the solid products the volcanoes have thrown off a long distance owing to the explosions in their craters. Scattered all over there are almost round rocks of different size, together with the spongy lapilli with their glossy surface made up by small grains 4-6 mm in diameter, as well as the ever-present ashes, that fine dust solidified in the atmosphere and blown by the wind from place to place, even to regions very far from the volcanoes.

The lower part of the Park is a spacious field of solidified lava whose surface is almost completely flat, only broken by the ruggedness of the volcanic crevices. Here there is a series of craters and volcanic cones from different ages that are the geological traces from a very intense volcanic past.

The Volcano of Caldera Roja (Red Cauldron) stands out quite distinctly on the northern limits of the Park. This volcano was developed in the course of a non-historical eruption; in the vicinities of this cone springs the only fresh water fountain of the Park. It is the fountain of «Los Miraderos» from which a continuous thread of water flows. In the chronicles of the island it is mentioned that prior to the eruptions of the 18th and 19th centuries there used to be many springs of fresh water that made this region have the most fertile land in the island. Today, this thin of thread of water that springs from deep in the earth is the only remainder from a near past when these valleys were lush and fertile.

The craters originated by the last eruptions are clearly outlined, with their layers of decolorized patches of blackish, brown, yellowish and reddish ashes and lapilli. All the craters have their own name and are different in shape, although they are all framed by the same landscape:

There are temperature of 400° Celsius at Montañas del Fuego.

Phenomenon of pressure steam jet caused by the high temperatures in the region.

Montaña de Fuego or Timanfaya, Caldera Bermeja (Red Cauldron), Los Miraderos, Caldera Rajada (Cracked Cauldron), Pedro Perico, Caldera de los Cuervos (Crows Cauldron), Montaña Encantada (Haunted Mountain), Pico Partido (Cracked Peak), and Montaña Rajada (Cracked Mountain). In some of these craters one can still see the solidified lava paths that one day came out from the volcanos like incandescent liquid rivers.

The Islet of Hilario has this name in memory of a man thus called who lived here in solitude accompanied by a camel. Here there is a restaurant, perhaps the only one in the world whose kitchen utilizes the heat given off by the volcanic soil. The appropriate name of this restaurant is «El Diablo» (The Devil). There are other services here as well as a small souvenir store. There are also continuous shows of the incredibly high temperatures that exist just a few centimeters below the floor one is standing on. These temperatures reach the 360° Celsius at only 6 meters deep, and are of 60° Celsius on the surface ground. The earth, or as the natives call it «Picón» (Sting), literally burns. If a few dry twigs are thrown into a small hole in the ground, after a moment they catch fire. If water is poured through one of the tubes expressly put there for the experiment, after a while a great noisy jet of water comes out; a true geyser has been made. Another unforgettable experience is to be here when one of the scarce showers happens to fall; it is then when everything is enveloped in

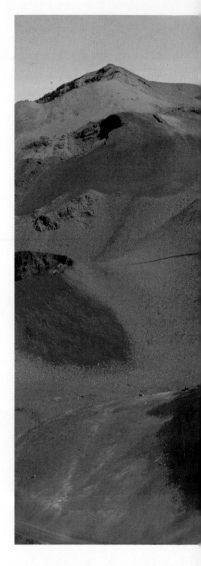

The Islet of Hilario
at Montañas del Fuego.

101

An impressive view of the creaters.

steam columns that cover the whole area.

A road that goes through the entire Park lies perfectly camouflaged within the landscape, without there being any exterior signs for its existence. This is the so-called «Ruta de los Volcanes» (Route of the Volcanoes). It extends for 14 kilometers and leads the visitors to the vicinities of the craters, allowing them to have a glimpse of truly apocalyptic landscapes. The route starts and ends at the Islet of Hilario. It is not permitted to go on it on foot or by private car; only the buses of the travel agencies can make the tour, as well as an express bus from the Council Hall that leaves every hour and offers the services of a tour guide that explains the sights in several languages.

The whole tour of this route takes approximately 50 minutes. There is a stop at Montaña Rajada (374 meters high) in the place known as El Mirador, from where most of the park and the entire coastline can be admired. After an almost science fiction landscape of continuous fields of lava, cragged gorges and the typical «malpaís», the visitors arrive at the «Valle de la Tranquilidad» (Tranquility Valley), an ample space whose surface appears like a carpet of ashes and lapilli offering a quite sober sight. Then comes Montaña de Fuego or Timanfaya, 510 meters above sea level. Here one can see the camels that bring the visitors along the road Yaiza-Tinajo and who preferred this unusual ride to the conventional bus. Finally the visitors arrive back at the islet of Hilario.

A must to the visitor following this route is to enjoy the diverse volcanic formations he will find along the way. There are narrow passes between walls of lava, oddshaped defiles, boulders of all sizes and diverse craters, constituting a hallucinating landscape in a world where the inanimate, bare matter takes the main role.

From the nine National Parks existing in Spain, this is the only one exclusively dedicated to the protection of unique geological formations. And here this is truly a unique, grandiose volcanis landscape. There are no trees to break the monochromatic, dark outline. The visitor cannot help feeling very small when he finds himself surrounded by all this overwhelming desolation.

The National Park of Timanfaya is, from a geomorphological point of view, an authentic museum where the complex volcanic processes can be studied in depth. All the evidence of volcanic life that exists here sometimes can even become too much: craters, volcanic cones, adjoining cones, lapilli, ashes and so on. The huge volcanic defiles, that stretch endlessly resemble the rough surface of a stormy sea. The surrounding natural landscape makes of this Park a place whose aesthetic worth stands hand in hand with that of the rest of the islands, and thus this touching barrenness becomes pictorial and sculpturesque.

Concerning the vegetable kingdom it must be said that although this is a land apparently desolate, some places are beginning to be

Tourists enjoying the camel tour of the Park.

colonized with plants. The species firstly chosen was the lichen, the perfect symbiosis of mushroom and alga. Today this is the plant most widely spread throughout the National Park. Thirty different species of lichen have been identified, although some specialists believe that the real number of species growing here is over one hundred. The lichen grows within the limits of the Park and has started to cover the hard volcanic rocks, painting them with soft specific tinges, mainly white-grayish and whitish hues.

It is surprising to see the number of higher plants existing in this exclusively geological territory, not only for the recent eruptions, but also for the adverse climatical conditions the plants must cope with, with the exception of the humidity at night, which is the only positive factor they enjoy. All the plants here are perfectly adapted to the extreme xerophilous conditions that exist in the Park.

There are 177 different species from 138 genera belonging to 42 families. There are three families endemic to Lanzarote: «Tojio», with showy, bright yellow flowers; «Lengua de Vaca» (Cow tongue) a boraginaceous with blue flowers and the «Salado Blanco», a small plant with woody twigs and almost white leaves.

There are also thirteen species endemic to the Canary Islands and nine that are Macaroneric endemic varieties. Among the Canarian endemic plants are the «berode», with wide, thick leaves and whitish flowers; the «ratonera» (Mousetrap), one of the most abundant species in the Park, and the «Romero» (Rosemary), a woody plant with whitishyellowish flowers. Another remarkable plant is the «corazoncillo» (Small heart), with trefoil leaves and yellow flowers.

Thirty six percent of all the species of vascular plants known in the Island of Lanzarote are found in the National Park. The greatest part of the botanical wealth grows in certain isolated sections known as «islotes»

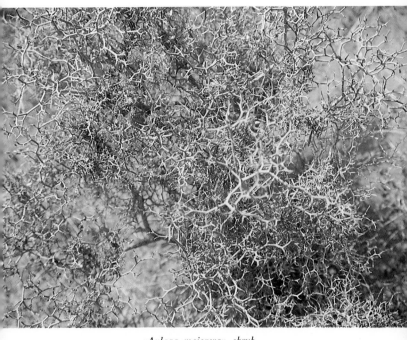

«Aulaga majorera» shrub.

(keys), whose ecological formation is more ancient, and in the lava fields and ash-covered areas. Some of the most important keys are those of Hilario, Timanfaya, Chinero, Montaña Bermeja, Montaña Tremesana and Montaña Halcónes.

Among the emphorbiaceous there are several «tabaibas» for instance the «sweet tabaiba» a very dangerous species that has grown well in these lava fields. Another common shrub is the «julaga» or «aulaga majorera» whose branches are publicly burnt for the visitors in the volcanic holes of the islet of Hilario.

Perhaps one of the most remarkable plants is the bulrush seen growing on the slopes of the volcanic cones

Bulrush.

that face the ocean. The bulrush plants grow so perfectly aligned that it seems as though if they were planted by an expert gardener. The presence of the bulrush, a plant that usually grows in very humid regions, can only be explained by the fact that as the soil consists of ashes and lapilli with great hydroscopic capacity, it condensates the atmospheric humidity, allowing this juncaceous plant to grow in this volcanic land.

The animal life of the National Park is quite meager, there being only a few birds and a reptile that lives in the holes of the rocks and is often seen basking motionless: the Lizard of Haria. This lacertilian, endemic to the eastern islands and islets of the Canarian Archipelago, is very small, for it does not surpass

Lichens.

the 20 centimeters in length. It has adapted itself to life in these hard, desolate volcanic territories. The female lizard produces two or three eggs once or twice per year. This, plus the fact of having no natural enemies has made it an abundant species in the Park. It is blackish or gray and feeds on insects and on the scarse plants it finds.

The coriaceous mass of the solidified lava is where the wild pigeon make its nests; this pigeon is often seen flying along the Route of the Volcanoes. Other birds are seen flying over the Park, but it is not known whether or not they nest here. Among these birds are the Ashen tern, the common «paiño», the falcon of Eleonor, the common turtledove, the one-colored martin, the black-headed «carruca», the common «mosquitero» and the common linnet.

The National Park lies 40 kilometers from Arrecife and 33 kilometers from the airport. It is recommended to take the road to Yaiza and from Yaiza take the road to Tinajo. Amidst a sea of lava the visitor gets to the limits of the Park, the departure point for the camel tours. Another road goes directly to the Islet of Hilario, and the road of Tinajo can be taken to return.

There are other interesting places in the island: Punta Fariones, where there is a lookout place wisely blended in the surrounding landscape offering a view of the island of Granciosa, and on a clear day, the Island of Alegranza. On the left stand the cliffs of Tamara, one of the areas with the widest variety of birds. In the vicinities of Masdache stands Montaña Blanca (White Mountain), worth visiting for its attractive landscape. The southern peninsula of the island is known as Punta

Hermitage of the Virgin of the Volcanoes.

The Beach of Famara, in front of the Island La Graciosa.

Papagayo (Parrot Cape). Another ineteresting attraction in the island is to make a tour of the fortresses of Lanzarote, which are of historical value.

Timanfaya is, in a few words, a region «without the seventh day of Creation», where the visitor can witness the aftermath of the inner turmoil of the earth in the midst of a scenery that makes him feel insignificant and removed to another world.

INDEX

INFORMACION PRACTICA
INFORMATION PRATIQUE
PRACTICAL INFORMATION
PRAKTISCHE HINWEISE

ARCHIPIELAGO CANARIO
ARCHIPEL DES CANARIES
THE CANARIES ARCHIPELAGO
DER KANARISCHE ARCHIPEL

Tenerife, Gran Canaria, La Palma, La Gomera, El Hierro, Fuerteventura y Lanzarote, con los islotes de Islas de Lobos, Alegranza, Graciosa, Roque del Este y Roque del Oeste.
Está dividido en dos provincias: Tenerife, La Palma, La Gomera y El Hierro, con SANTA CRUZ DE TENERIFE como capital.
Y Gran Canaria, Fuerteventura, Lanzarote e islotes, con LAS PALMAS DE GRAN CANARIA como capital.

Posición geográfica:

27° 44'-29° 15' latitud N. y 13° 26'-17° 53' longitud W.

Altura máxima del Archipiélago.

Pico del Teide, 3.716 m.
Extensión superficial: 7.543 km. cuadrados.
Extensión de la provincia de Santa Cruz de Tenerife: 3.444 km. cuadrados.
Extensión de la isla de Tenerife: 2.058 km²
Habitantes en la isla de Tenerife: 560.000.
Distancias en millas desde el puerto de Santa Cruz de Tenerife a los de las otras islas y costas de Africa:

A las Palmas de Gran Canaria	54
A Santa Cruz de La Palma	102
A Arrecife (Lanzarote)	186
A San Sebastián de La Gomera	153
A Puerto del Rosario (Fuert.)	156
A Valverde (El Hierro)	156
A Cabo Juby (Costa de Africa)	180

Tenerife es un triángulo cuyos vértices son: Punta de Anaga (vértice NE), Punta de Teno (vértice NW) y Punta de la Rasca (vértice S).
Lado mayor: Anaga-Teno, 80 km.
Lado menor: Rasca-Teno, 45 km.

Ténérife, Grande Canarie, La Palma, La Gomera, El Hierro, Fuerteventura et Lanzarote avec les îlots de Islas de Lobos, Alegranza, Graciosa, Roque del Este et Roque del Oeste. Il est divisé en deux provinces: Tenerife, La Palma, La Gomera et El Hierro avec SANTA CRUZ DE TENERIFE comme capitale.
Et La Grande Canarie, Fuerteventura, Lanzarote et les îlots avex LAS PALMAS DE GRAN CANARIA comme capitale.

Position géographique:

27° 44'-29° 15' latitude Nord et 13° 26'-17° 53' longitude Ouest.

Altitude maximum de l'archipel:

Pic du Teide, 3716 mètres.
Extension: 7543 km²
Extension de la province de Santa Cruz de Ténérife: 3444 km².
Extension de l'île de Ténérife: 2058 km².
Habitants de l'île de Ténérife: 560000.
Distances en milliers de km entre le port de Santa Cruz de Tenerife et ceux des autres îles et côtes d'Afrique:

A Las Palmas de Gran Canaria	*54*
A Santa Cruz de La Palma	*102*
A Arrecife (Lanzarote)	*186*
A San Sebastián de La Gomera	*153*
A Puerto del Rosario (Fuertev.)	*156*
A Valverde (El Hierro)	*156*
A Cabo Juby (Côte d'Afrique)	*180*

Ténérife a la forme d'un triangle dont les sommets sont:
Punta de Anaga (sommet NE) Punta de Teno (NO) Punta de la Rasca (Sud).
Plus grand côté: Anaga-Teno 80 km.
Plus petit côté: Rasca-Teno 45 km.

It consists of Tenerife, Gran Canaria, La Palma, La Gomera, El Hierro, Fuerteventura and Lanzarote together with the small islands Islas de Lobos, Alegranza, Graciosa, Roque del Este and Roque del Oeste.

It is divided into two provinces: Tenerife, La Palma, La Gomera and El Hierro, whose capital is SANTA CRUZ DE TENERIFE, and Gran Canaria, Fuerteventura, Lanzarote and the small islands, whose capital is LAS PALMAS DE GRAN CANARIA.

Geographical Position

27° 44'-29° 15' Latitude N. and 13° 26'-17° 53' Longitude W.

Highest point of the Archipelago:

Pico del Teide, 3,716 metres.
Surface area: 7,543 sq. kilometres.
Surface area of the province of Santa Cruz de Tenerife: 3,444 sq. km.
Surface area of Tenerife Island: 2,058 sq. km.
Population of Tenerife Island: 560.000.
Some distances from the port of Santa Cruz de Tenerife (in miles):

Las Palmas de Gran Canaria	54
Santa Cruz de La Palma	102
Arrecife (Lanzarote)	186
San Sebastián de La Gomera	153
Puerto del Rosario (Fuertv.)	156
Valverde (El Hierro)	156
Cabo Juby (African Coast)	180

Tenerife is a triangle whose vertices are Anaga Point (North-east), Teno Point (North-west), and Rasca Point (South).
Longest side: Anaga-Teno, 80 km.
Shortest side: Rasca-Teno, 45 km.

Der kanarische Archipel besteht aus folgenden Inseln: Teneriffa, Gran Canaria, La Palma, La Gomera, El Hie ro, Fuerteventura und Lanzarote mit dem kleinen Inseln Islas de Lobos, Alegranza, Graciosa, Roque del Este und Roque del Oeste.

Dei inselgruppe gliedert sich in zwei Provinzen: Tenerife, La Palma, La Gomera und El Hierro mit SANTA CRUZ DE TENERIFE als Hauptstadt, Gran Canaria, Fuerteventura, Lanzarote und kleine Inseln mit LAS PALMAS DE GRAN CANARIA als Hauptstadts:

Geographische Lage:

27° 44'-29° 15' Breitengrand N und 13° 26'-17° 53' Längengrand W.

Hochstpunkt des Archipels:

Pico del Teide 3.716 m.
Oberfläche: 7.543 qkm.
Oberfläche der Provinz von Santa Cruz de Tenerife: 3.444 qkm.
Oberfläche der Insein Teneriffa: 2.058 qkm.
Einwohnerzahl der Inseln Teneriffa: 560.000.
Entfernungen in Meilen vom Hafen Santa Cruz de Tenerife zu den Häfen der anderen Inseln und Küsten Afrikas:

Nach Las Palmas de Gran Canaria	54
Nach Santa Cruz de La Palma	102
Nach Arrecife (Lanzarote)	186
Nach San Sebastián auf La Gomera	153
Nach Puerto del Rosario (Fuerteventura)	156
Nach Valverde (El Hierro)	156
Nach Kap Juby (Küste Afrikas)	180

Teneriffa is ein Dreieck, dessen Ekken folgande Landzungen bilden: Punta de Anaga (NO-Ecke). Punta de Teno (NW-Ecke) und Punta de la Rasca (S-Ecke).
Längste Seite: Anaga-Teno 80 km.
Kürzeste Seite: Rasca-Teno 45 km.

ARTE Y CULTURA
ART ET CULTURE
ART AND CULTURE
KUNST UND KULTUR

CONJUNTO MONUMENTAL
ENSEMBLE MONUMENTAL
MONUMENTS
SEHENSWURDIGKEITEN

Santa Cruz de Tenerife

CASTILLO DE PASO ALTO.
CHATEAU DE PASO ALTO.
PASO ALTO CASTLE.
BURG PASO ALTO.

Monumento a los héroes del 25 de mayo de 1797 (victoria sobre el almirante Nelson). Puede verse en este museo militar el cañón «Tigre», una de cuyas balas arrancó el brazo del almirante inglés.

Monument aux héros du 25 mai 1797 (victoire sur l'Amiral Nelson). Dans ce musée militaire on peut voir le canon «Tigre», l'une des balles duquel arracha le bras de l'amiral anglais.

Monument to the heroes of 25th May 1797 (victory over Admiral Nelson). In the military museum, visitors can see the cannon «Tigre», one of the balls from which took off the English Admiral's arm.

Ein Denkmal für die Helden des 25. Mai 1797 (Sieg über den Admiral Nelson). In diesen Militärmuseum ist die Kanone «Tiger» zu sehen, von deren Kugeln eine den Arm des englischen Generals abriss.

IGLESIA DE LA CONCEPCION.
EGLISE DE LA CONCEPTION.
CHURCH OF LA CONCEPCION.
KIRCHE «LA CONCEPCION».

Construida en el siglo XVI y reconstruida después de un incendio en el XVII, es el templo más importante, en cuyas cinco naves se guardan interesantes muestras del estilo barroco y los más valiosos recuerdos históricos de las Canarias. Aquí se conserva la Cruz de la Conquista y las banderas arrebatadas al almirante Nelson, con motivo de su frustrado ataque a la plaza. La Capilla de Carta, prodigio de talla en madera a mano, y la hermosa sillería de coro, hoy instalada en el presbiterio, son también de interés artístico.

Construite au 16e s. et reconstruite après un incendie au 17e, c'est le temple le plus important. Dans ses cinq nefs on montre d'intéressantes traces du style baroque et des souvenirs historiques de la plus grande valeur des îles Canaries. On conserve ici la Croix de la Conquête et les drapeaux arrachés à l'amiral Nelson, lors de son attaque frustré à la place. La Capilla de Carta, chef-d'oeuvre de sculpture de bois à la main, et la belle stalle du choeur, installée aujourd'hui au presbitérium, sont également d'intérêt artistique.

Built in the 16th century and rebuilt after a fire in the 17th, it is the biggest church and in its aisles can be found some interesting examples of the Baroque style and some valuable historical relics of the past of the Canary Islands. Here, the Cross of the Conquest is preserved, as well as the colours taken from Admiral Nelson during his unsuccessful attack on the fortress. The Carta Chapel, which is a Magnificent example of woodcarving, and the beautiful choir stalls are also of artistic interest.

117

Erbaut im 16. Jahrhundert und rekonstruiert nach einem Brand im 17. Jahrhundert, ist sie die bedeutendste Kirche, in deren fünf Schiffen interessante Zeugnisse des Barockstils und die wertvollsten historischen Erinnerungen der Kanarischen Inseln aufbewahrt werden. Hier befinden sich das Kreuz der Eroberung und die dem Admiral Nelson bei seinem vergeblichen Angriff auf den Platz abgenommenen Fahnen. Die Carta-Kapelle, eine wundervolle Handschnitzerei, und das prächtige Chorgestühl, das heute im Altarraum steht, sind ebenfalls von künstlerischem Interesse.

IGLESIA DE SAN FRANCISCO.
EGLISE DE SAN FRANCISCO.
THE CHURCH OF SAN FRANCISCO.
KIRCHE DES HEILIGEN FRANZISKUS.

Portada barroca del siglo XVIII con columnas salomónicas. Son notables las imágenes de San Pedro de Alcántara, del mismo siglo, y el Señor de las Tribulaciones.

Son frontispice est baroque du 18e s. avec des colonnes salomon. Les images de Saint Pierre d'Alcántara, du même siècle, et le Seigneur des Tribulations, sont remarquables.

18th century Baroque façade with spiral columns. Also noteworthy are the images of Saint Peter of Alcántara, from the same century, and of the Christ of Tribulations.

Barockportal aus dem 18. Jahrhundert mit Salomonsäulen. Beachtlich sind die Bilder des Heiligen Petrus von Alcántara aus demselben Jahrhundert und des Hern der Drangsal.

MONUMENTO A LOS CAIDOS.
MONUMENT AUX MORTS.
MEMORIAL TO THE FALLEN.
GEFALLENENDENKMAL.

Artístico monumento con esbelta torre, provisto de ascensor que lleva a la parte alta.

C'est un artistique monument avec une tour élancée, munie d'un ascensour qui conduit au sommet.

An artistic monument with a slender tower, equipped with a lift to take visitors to the top.

Artistisches Denkmal mit schlankem Turm, mit einem Aufzug, der in den oberen Teil führt.

MONUMENTO A LA CANDELARIA.
MONUMENT A LA CANDELARIA.
MONUMENT TO OUR LADY OF LA CANDELARIA.
DENKMAL DER MARIA REINIGUNG.

Simboliza la Adoración de la Virgen, Patrona del Archipiélago, por los guanches, primitivos pobladores. Este monumento fue construido en mármol de Carrara en 1718 y es debido al famoso escultor Casanova.

Symbolise la vénération des habitants primitifs, les guanches, pour la Vierge, patronne de l'Archipel. Le monument fut construit en 1718, en marbre de Carrare, par le fameux sculpteur Casanova.

It symbolizes the Adoration of the Virgin Mary, Patron Saint of the Archipelago, by the Guanches, the original inhabitants of the islands. It was built of Carrara marble in 1718 and is attributed to the famous sculptor Cassanova.

Ein Symbol für die Anbetung der Jungfrau, der Schutzherrin der Inselgruppe, durch die Guanchen, die ursprünglichen Bewohner Dieses Denkmal wurde aus Carrara-Marmor 1718 errichtet und ist dem berühmten Bildhauer Casanova zu verdanken.

PALACIO DE CARTA. *PALAIS DE CARTA.*
PALACE OF CARTA. *PALAST VON CARTA.*

Siglo XVIII. Característica arquitectura canaria mezclada con elementos mudéjares y flamencos.

XVIII siècle. Architecture canarienne caractéristique mêlée à des éléments mudéjars et flamands.

18th century. Characteristic Canary architecture mixed with Mudejar and Flemish elements.

XVIII. Jahrhundert. Charakteristische kanarische Architektur durchsetzt mit mudejar und flaemischen Elementen.

PALACIO INSULAR.
PALAIS INSULAIRE.
THE ISLAND PALACE.
INSELPALAST.

Moderno edificio de majestuosa traza, donde pueden admirarse unas magníficas pinturas de José Aguiar.

C'est un édifice moderne de prestance majestueuse et où l'on peut admirer de magnifiques peintures de José Aguiar.

A modern building with majestic lines, where visitors may admire the magnificent paintings of Jose Aguiar.

Ein majestätisch angelegtes, modernes Gebäude, wo grossartige Gemälde von José Aguiar bewundert werden können.

La Laguna

IGLESIA DE SAN FRANCISCO.
EGLISE DE SAN FRANCISCO.
THE CHURCH OF SAN FRANCISCO.
KIRCHE DES HEILIGEN FRANZISKUS.

Donde se venera con gran devoción el Santísimo Cristo de la Laguna. Esta imagen es una tabla esbozada en madera de bornio de fines del XV, en tamaño natural, atribuido a un artista anónimo de la escuela sevillana. La imagen fue traida a Tenerife por el Adelantado D. Alonso Fernández de Lugo.

On y vénère avec grande dévotion le Christ de La Laguna. Cette image est une planche étuvée en bois de la fin du 16ᵉ s. et de taille humaine; on l'attribue à un artiste anonyme de l'école sévillane. L'image fut transportée à Ténérife par l'amiral Alonso Fernández de Lugo.

Where the Christ of La Laguna is venerated with great devotion. The life-sized image is of decorated wood and is attributed to an anonymous artist of the Seville School of the late 15th century. It was brought to Tenerife by Governor Alonso Fernández de Lugo.

Dort wird mit grosser Hingabe der Allerheiligste Christus der Laguna verehrt. Dieses Bild ist ein in Holz gearbeitetes Tafelbild vom Ende des 15. Jahrhunderts in natürlicher Grösse, das einem anonymen Künstler der Schule von Sevilla zugeschrieben wird. Das Bild wurde von dem Gouverneur Alonso Fernández de Lugo nach Teneriffa gebracht.

CATEDRAL. *CATHEDRALE.*
CATHEDRAL. *KATHEDRALE.*

Edificio con esbeltez equilibrada y en justa proporción sus columnas, arcos y bóvedas. El ábside es muy hermoso; su presbiterio, construido sobre cuatro gradas de mármol, es de inconfundible aire neogótico. El coro, legado por el arzobispo Bencomo, es neoclásico, como el trazado de la fachada. Dentro de este coro hay un facístol y en él, un pequeño crucifijo de Domingo Estévez. También puede admirarse el espléndido órgano construido en Londres, en 1857. En la capilla de los Remedios hay un retablo barroco de principios del siglo XVIII.

C'est un édifice svelte et bien proportionné dans ses colonnes, ses arcs et ses voûtes. L'abside est très belle; le presbyterium, construit sur quatre marches de marbre, est d'un estyle néogothique. Le choeur, don de l'archevêque Bencomo, est néoclassique, de même que le frontispice. Dans le choeur il y a un lutrin dominé par un petit crucifix de Domingo Estévez.

On peut y admirer également un orgue splendide, construit à Londres en 1857. Dans la chapelle des Remedios il existe un retable baroque du 18ᵉ s.

A building whose slenderness is balanced and whose columns, arches and vaults are in correct proportion. The apse is extremely beautiful, while its presbytery, built on top of four marble steps has an unmistakable neo-Gothic air about it. The choir, a legacy from Archbishop Bencomo, is neo-Classical, as is the layout of the façade. Within this choir, there is a lectern on which there is a small crucifix by Domingo Estévez. Visitors can also admire the splendid organ which was built in London in 1857. In the Los Remedios Chapel, there is a Baroque altarpiece from the early 18th century.

Ein Gebäude von ausgeglichener schlanker Form, dessen Säulen, Bögen und Gewölberichtig proportioniert sind. Die Apsis ist sehr schön; sein Altarraum, errichtet auf vier Marmorstufen, hat ein unverkennbar neugotisches Aussehen. Der Chor, ein Legat des Erzbischofs Bencomo, ist neuklassisch, wie die Fassade. In diesem Chor befindet sich ein Chorpult und darin ein kleines Kruzifix von Domingo Estévez. Ebenfalls ist die herrliche, 1857 in London gebaute Orgel zu bewundern. In der Remedios-Kapelle befindet sich ein barockes Altarbild vom Anfang des 18. Jahrhunderts.

PALACIO DEL CABILDO.
PALAIS DU CABILDO.
THE CABILDO PALACE.
PALAST DES STADTRATES.

Se comenzó a construir en 1542; en su puerta, de estilo plateresco en piedra rosa, triunfan las armas de Carlos V y del Regidor Alvárez de Sotomayor.

On commença sa construction en 1542; sur sa porte, de style platéresque en pierre rose, figurent les armes de Charles-Quint et de l'échevin Alvarez de Sotomayor.

This building was begun in 1542; on its door, in pink stone in the plateresque style, can be seen the coats-of-arms of Carlos V and Alderman Alvarez de Sotomayor.

1542 wurde mit seinem Bau begonnem; auf seinem Tor, in platereskem Stil aüs rosa Stein, heben sich die Wappen von Karl V. und dem Stadtrat Alvarez de Sotomayor ab.

LA CONCEPCION. *LA CONCEPCION.*
LA CONCEPCION. *LA CONCEPCION.*

Gótica con elementos mudéjares. Principios del siglo XVI. Varias reformas, la más importante

119

del siglo XVIII. Coros y púlpitos barrocos, magníficos.

Gothique avec éléments mudéjars. Début du XVI siècle. Plusieurs réformes, la plus importante au XVIII siècle. Choeurs et chaires magnifiques.

Gothic with Mudejar elements. Beginning of the 16th century. Several reformations, the most important in the 18th century. Baroque choirs and pulpits magnificent.

Gotisch mit mudejar Elementen. Anfang des XVI. Jahrhundert Verschiedene Aenderungen, die Wichtigste im XVIII. Jahrhundert. Choere und Kanzeln barok, praechtig.

PALACIO DE LOS CONDES DE SALAZAR.
PALAIS DES COMTES DE SALAZAR.
PALACE OF THE COUNTS OF SALAZAR.
PALAST DER GRAFEN VON SALAZAR.

Construido en el siglo XVII, en él se compaginan la suntuosidad y la gracia dados los ricos artesonados de sus interiores. En la actualidad se encuentra instalado aquí el Obispo.

Construit au 17e s., réunit à la fois, la somptuosité et la grâce de sa riche voûte à caissons. Actuellement l'Evêque réside là.

Built in the 17th century, it combines magnificence and grace in its priceless coffered ceilings. At present it is the Bishop's Residence.

Erbaut im 17. Jahrhundert. In ihm verbindet sich Prunk und Grazie durch das Täfelwerk in seinem Inneren. Gegenwärtig ist es der Bischofssitz.

PALACIO DE LOS VILLANUEVA DEL PRADO.
PALAIS DES VILLANUEVA DEL PRADO.
THE VILLANUEVA DEL PRADO PALACE.
PALAST DER VILLANUEVA DEL PRADO.

Reedificado a mediados del siglo XVIII, pleno de lujo y elegancia, fue sede de una famosísima tertulia erudita —1760 a 1770— que marcó surcos intelectuales y cuyo director fue el famoso historiador don Joseph de Viera y Clavijo.

Reconstruit au milieu du 18e s. plein de luxe et d'élégance, il fut le siège d'une fort fameuse réunion d'érudits —1760-1770— qui laisse des traces durables et dont le directeur fut le fameux historien Joseph de Viera y Clavijo.

Rebuilt in the middle of the 18th century, it is both luxurious and elegant. Between 1760 and 1770, it was a famous meeting place for the learned minds of the period, who blazed new trails in thinking under the leadership of the renowned historian, Joseph de Viera y Clavijo.

Neuerbaut Mitte des 18. Jahrhunderts, voller Luxus und Eleganz, war er Sitz eines berühmten Stammtisches von Gelehrten —1760 bis 1770— der intellektuelle Spuren hinterliess und dessen Leiter der berühmte Geschichtsschreiber Joseph de Viera y Clavijo war.

Puerto de La Cruz

ACANTILADO MARTIAÑEZ.
ACANTILADO MARTIAÑEZ.
THE MARTIAÑEZ CLIFFS.
STEILKÜSTE MARTIAÑEZ.

Lugar donde moraban los antiguos guanches y desde donde se divisa todo el término municipal de Puerto de La Cruz.

Lieu où habitaient les anciens guanches et d'où l'on contemple toute la commune du Puerto de La Cruz.

These were inhabited by the ancient Guanche peoples and from it the whole of Puerto de La Cruz can be seen.

Wohnort der ehemaligen Guanchen, von wo aus der ganze Bezirk Puerto de La Cruz zu sehen ist.

CASTILLO DE SAN FELIPE.
CHATEAU DE SAN FELIPE.
SAN FELIPE CASTLE.
BURG SAN FELIPE.

Antiguo fuerte junto al mar.

Ancien fort face à la mer.

An old fort on the shore.

Ehemalige Burg am Meer.

IGLESIA DE NUESTRA SEÑORA DE LA PEÑA DE FRANCIA.
EGLISE DE NOTRE-DAME DE LA PEÑA DE FRANCIA.
CHURCH OF OUR LADY OF THE PEÑA DE FRANCIA.
KIRCHE «NUESTRA SEÑORA DE LA PEÑA DE FRANCIA».

Construida en 1603, aquí se veneran las imágenes de Cristo del Gran Poder y de la Virgen del Carmen, patronos de la población.

Construite en 1603, on y vénère les images du Christ del Gran Poder et de la Vierge del Carmen, patronne de la ville.

Built in 1603, the images of Christ the Almighty and Our Lady of Mount Carmel, patron saints of the town are venerated here.

Erbaut 1603. Hier werden die Bilder des Allmächtigen Christus und der Jungfrau des Carmen verehrt, der Schutzheiligen des Ortes.

La Orotava

LA CONCEPCION.
LA CONCEPCION.
LA CONCEPCION.
LA CONCEPCION.

Siglo XVIII. Sigue el tipo de basílica florentina de Brunelleschi. Tabernáculo neoclásico.

XVIII siècle. Suit le type de basilique florentine de Brunelleschi. Tabernacle néoclassique.

18th century. Like Brunelleschi type florentine basilica. Neoclassical tabernacle.

XVIII. Jahrhundert. Folgt dem Typ der florentinischen Basilika von Brunelleschi Neuklassischer Tabernakel.

Santa Cruz de La Palma

AYUNTAMIENTO. *MAIRIE.*
TOWN HALL. *RATHAUS.*

Construido en 1563, es estilo renacimiento italiano. Todos los elementos de la construcción y ornamentación exterior son curiosamente asimétricos, pero tan armoniosamente conjuntados, que es necesario fijar la atención en el detalle para reparar en la asimetría.

Construite en 1563 en style renaissance italienne. Tous les éléments de la construction et de l'ornementation extérieure sont curieusement assymétriques, mais assemblés de telle manière qu'il faut prêter attention au détail pour en remarquer l'assymétrie.

Built in 1563 in the Italian Renaissance style. All the outside constructional and decorative elements are curiously asymmetrical and yet they are so harmoniously combined that it is necessary to carry out a detailed examination to notice this asymmetry.

Erbaut 1563, in italienischen Renaissancestil. Alle äusseren Bau und Zierelemente sind seltsam asymmetrisch, jedoch so harmonisch verbunden, dass man seine Aufmerksamkeit auf Einzelheiten richten muss, um die Asymmetrie wahrzunehmen.

PARROQUIA DEL SALVADOR.
PAROISSE DU SAUVEUR.
THE PARISH CHURCH OF EL SALVADOR.
PFARRKIRCHE DES «SALVADOR».

Es una de las construcciones religiosas más armoniosas y elegantes del Archipiélago. El pórtico, de cantería labrada, es de estilo renacentista. El artesonado, mudéjar. El techo de la sacristía, gótico, único ejemplar en la isla.

C'est l'une des constructions religieuses les plus élégantes et harmonieuses de l'Archipel. Le portique, en pierre taillée, est de style renaissance. La voûte à caissons est mudéjar, et le plafond de la sacristie, gothique, est un exemple unique dans toute l'île.

This is one of the most harmonious and elegant religious buildings in the Archipelago. The portico of dressed stonework is in the Renaissance style, the coffered ceilings are Mudejar, while the ceiling of the sacristy is Gothic, the only example of this style on the island.

Sie ist eine der harmonischsten und elegantesten kirchlichen Bauten des Archipels. Das Portal aus behauenem Stein ist Renaissancestil, das Täfelwerk Mudejar stil, die Decke der Sakristei gotisch, das einzige Beispiel dafür auf der Insel.

CASTILLO DE SANTA CATALINA.
CHATEAU DE SANTA CATALINA.
SANTA CATALINA CASTLE.
BURG VON SANTA CATALINA.

Siglo XVI. Reconstruido el siglo XVII. Planta cuadrada con cuatro baluartes en ángulo.

XVI siècle. Reconstruit au XVII siècle. Plan carré avec quatre bastions dans les angles.

16th century. Reconstructed in the 17th century. Square plan with four angular bastions.

XVI. Jahrhundert. Wiederaufgebaut im XVII. Jahrhundert. Viereckiger Grundriss mit vier Basteien an den Ecken.

Las Palmas

CATEDRAL. *CATHÉDRALE.*
CATHEDRAL. *KATHEDRALE.*

Comenzada a construir en 1497, de estilo gótico, contiene un rico tesoro de ornamentos litúrgicos y de cuadros. En ella se custodia el Pendón de la Conquista. Entre sus obras más valiosas figura un portapaz, obra de Benvenuto Cellini, así como varias imágenes talladas por el escultor canario Luján Pérez, un cuadro del pintor Roelas y otro del Divino Morales.

On commença sa construction en 1497 en style gothique et elle garde un riche trésor en ornements liturgiques et en tableaux. On y garde l'Étendard de la Conquête. Parmi les plus précieuses oeuvres d'art figure une patène due à Benvenuto Cellini, ainsi que quelques sculptures taillées par l'artiste canarien Luján Pérez, un tableau du peintre Roelas et un autre de Morales.

Its construction was initiated in 1497. It has a Gothic style and contains a rich treasure of liturgic ornaments and paintings. The Standard of the Conquest is kept here. Among its most valuable works is a pix of Benvenuto Cellini, and various engraved statues by the Canary sculptor Luján Pérez, a painting by the Painter Roelas, and one by the Divine Morales.

Gotischer Bau, 1497 begonnen, mit wertuoller Schatzsammlung liturgischer Gewänder und Bilder. Aufbewahrungsort der Wiedereroberungsstandarte. Zu den wertvollsten Werken gehört ein Portapaz von Benvenuto Cellini, sowie verschiedene vom kanarischen Bildhauer Luján Pérez gefertigte Statuen, ein Bild des Malers Roelas und ein wei eres von Divino Morales.

ERMITA DE SAN ANTONIO ABAD
ERMITAGE DE SAINT ANTOINE ABBÉ (San Antonio Abad)
HERMITAGE OF ST. ANTHONY ABAD
KAPELLE DES ABTES SAN ANTONIO

Plaza de San Antonio Abad. Obra del siglo XVII levantada en el solar del templo en que estuvo situada la iglesia en la cual, según tradición, oró Cirstóbal Colón en el viaje del Descubrimiento.

Plaza de San Antonio Abad. Oeuvre du XVII°'s. érigé sur le terrain du temple où se trouvait située l'église dans laquelle, selon la tradition, Christophe Colomb pria lors du voyage de la Découverte.

Plaza de San Antonio Abad. A work of the XVII century which was built on the lot where, according to tradition, the church was located in which Christopher Columbus prayed on his way to Discover America.

Plaza de San ·Antonio Abad. Bau aus dem 17. jahrhundert, auf dem selben Grundstück errichtet auf dem früher die Kirche stand in der, laut Überlieferung, Christoph Kolumbus auf seiner Entdeckungsreise betete.

CEMENTERIO VIEJO
VIEUX CIMETIÈRE
OLD CEMENTERY
ALTER FRIEDHOF

Avenida Marítima del Sur. Puede admirarse en él la tumba del poeta Tomás Morales, obra de Victorio Macho.

Avda. Marítima del Sur. On peut y admirer la tombe du poète Tomás Morales, oeuvre de Victorio Macho.

Avda. Marítima del Sur. Here one can admire the tomb of the poet Tomás Morales, a work by Victorio Macho.

Avenida Marítima del Sur. Dort befindet sich das Grabmal des Dichters Tomás Morales, das ein Werk von Victorio Macho ist.

BARRIO DE VEGUETA
BARRIO DE VEGUETA
VEGUETA SECTOR
VEGUETA-VIERTEL

Se trata del barrio más antiguo de la ciudad, notable por el carácter de sus edificios, en los que la arquitectura colonial hispánica da sus primeros vagidos.

Il s'agit du quartier le plus ancien de la ville, remarquable pour le caractère de ses édifices, où l'architecture coloniale hispanique fit ses premiers pas.

This is the oldest neighborhood of the city, notable for the nature of its buildings which show signs of the Hispanic colonial architectural style.

Es handelt sich hier um das äteste Viertel der Stadt; seine Gebäude sind besonders interessant, da man hier die Anfänge der spanischen Kolonialarchitektur beobachten kann.

CASTILLO DE LA LUZ
CHÂTEAU DE LA LUZ
CASTLE OF LIGHT
LICHTERSCHLOSS

Bastión de la resistencia canaria contra. los ataques de los piratas en el siglo XVI. Está situado al fondo de la antigua dársena y ha sido declarado Monumento Histórico.

Bastion de la resistence canarienne contre les attaques des pirates du XVIème siècle. Il se trouve au fond du vieil arrière-port et il a été déclaré Monument Historique.

The Canary bastion of resistence against the pirate attacks of the XVI century. It lies at the bottom of the ancient dock and has been declared a Historic Monument.

Bollwerk des kanarischen Widerstands gegen Angriffe der Piraten im XVI Jahrhundert. Es liegt am .Ende des alten Hafenbeckens und wird als historisches. Denkmal bezeichnet.

Lanzarote

CASTILLO DE SAN GABRIEL
CHÂTEAU DE SAINT GABRIEL
CASTLE OF SAINT GABRIEL
SCHLOSS DES HL. GABRIELS

Se levanta en un islote frente al casco de la ciudad, reconstruido en 1590 por Torriani para defender Arrecife contra los continuos ataques de los piratas berberiscos. Está unido a la ciudad por un puente levadizo, llamado de «Las Bolas», y jugó su papel en las aventuras y piraterías de los siglos XV, XVI y XVII.

Il s'élève sur un îlot, face à la ville, reconstruit en 1590 par Torriani, pour défendre Arrecife contre les continuels attaques des pirates mauresques. Il est uni à la ville par un pont-levis, appelé de «Las Bolas» (Les Boules), et il eut son rôle dans les aventures et les pirateries des XVème, XVIème et XVIIème siècles.

This is built on an small island facing the town centre and was rebuilt in 1590 by Torriani to protect Arrecife against the continuous attacks by the Berber pirates. It is joined to the town by a lifting bridge called «Las Bolas» and played its part in the adventures and piracys of the XV, XVI and XVII centuries.

Es erhebt sich auf einem Eiland dem Stadtkern gegenüber. 1590 wurde es wiedererbaut zum Schutze von Arrecife gegen die ständigen. Angriffe der Berberpiraten. Eine Zugbrücke «Las Bolas» verbindet das Schloss mit der Stadt; sie spielte eine wichtige Rolle bei den abenteuerlichen Seeräuberüberfällen in XV XVI und XVII. Jahrhundert.

CASTILLO DE SAN JOSÉ
CHÂTEAU DE SAINT JOSEPH
CASTLE OF SAINT JOSEPH
SCHLOSS DES HL. JOSEPH

Construido en el año 1779 por orden del rey Carlos III. También es digna de ser visitada la iglesia parroquial de San Ginés, patrona de la Isla.

Construit dans l'année 1779, sur l'ordre du Roi Charles III. L'église paroissiale de San Ginés, Patron de l'île, est aussi digne d'être visitée.

Built in 1779 by order of King Charles III. The Parish church of Saint Ginés, the Island's Patron Saint, also deserves a visit.

1779 auf Geheiss König Karl III erbaut. Besuchenswert ist auch die Pfarrkirche der Hl. Ginés, der Inselpatronin.

Fuerteventura

CASA DE LOS CORONELES
MAISON DES COLONELS
HOUSE OF THE COLONELS
HAUS DER OBERSTEN

En la Oliva y entre sus viejos edificios se encuentra esta Casa, considerada como la más representativa construcción del siglo XVIII en el archipiélago.

Dans La Oliva, et parmi ses vieux édifices, on trouve cette Maison considerée comme la construction la plus représentative du XVIIIème siècle dans l'archipel.

In the village of Oliva, and amid its old buildings one con find this House which is considered as the best representative construction of the XVIII century in the Archipelago.

Das Haus befindet sich in La Oliva, umgeben von dessen alten Gebäuden. Allgemein betrachtet man es als das representativste Gebaäude aus dem XVIII Jahrhundert auf dem Archipel.

MUSEOS
MUSEÉS
MUSEUMS
MUSEUM

Santa Cruz de Tenerife

MUSEO ARQUEOLOGICO.
MUSEE ARCHEOLOGIQUE.
ARCHEOLOGICAL MUSEUM.
ARCHAEOLOGISCHES MUSEUM.
Calle Bravo Murillo, s./n.

Contenido: Arqueología y Antropología canaria.

Contenu: Archéologie et Anthropologie des ca-
naries.

Contents: Archeology and anthropology (Canary).

Inhalt: Archaeologie und janarische Anthro-
pologie.

MUSEO MUNICIPAL «Antiguo Convento de San
Francisco».
MUSEE MUNICIPAL. «Ancien Couvent de San
Francisco».
MUNICIPAL MUSEUM. «Antiguo Convento de
San Francisco».
STAEDTICHES MUSEUM. «Antiguo Convento
de San Francisco».
Calle J. Murphy, s/n.

Contenido: Exclusivamente dedicado a pintura
antigua, moderna y sobre todo local.

Contenu: Exclusivement dédié à la peinture, an-
cienne, moderne et surtout locale.

Contents: Dedicated exclusively to paintings;
old, modern and above all local.

Inhalt: Ausschliesslich der alten, modernen und
vor allem der lokalen Malerei gewidmet.

Las Palmas

MUSEO PROVINCIAL DE BELLAS ARTES
MUSÉE PROVINCIAL DE BEAUX-ARTS
PROVINCIAL MUSEUM OF FINE ARTS
LANDESMUSEUM DER SCHÖNEN KÜNSTE

Instalado en el mismo edificio de la Casa de
Colón. En él puede admirarse obras de los
más importantes artistas canarios, así como
tambien lienzos y esculturas de célebres
maestros españoles, sobre todo contempo-
ráneos, tales como Regoyos, Solana, Manolo
Hugué, etc.

Installé dans l'édifice même de la Casa de Co-
lón. On peut y admirer des oeuvres des plus
importants artistes canariens, ainsi que des
tableaux et des sculptures de célèbres maîtres
espagnols, surtout contemporains, tels que
Regoyos, Solana, Manolo Hugué, etc.

Installed in the same building as the House of
Columbus. One can admire works by the
most important artists of the Canary Islands,
as well as canvases and sculptures by famous Spanish masters, especially contempo-
rary ones such as Regoyos, Solana, Manolo
Hugué, etc.

Befindet sich in dem selben Gebäude wie das
Haus des Kolumbus. Dort kann man die be-
deutendsten Werke kanarischer Künstler be-
wundern und es befinden sich dort auch Öl-
gemälde und Skulpturen von berühmten
spanischen Meistern, vor allem von zeitge-
nössischen, wie Regoyos, Solana, Manolo
Hugué, u. a.

MUSEO CANARIO
MUSÉE CANARIEN
CANARY MUSEUM
KANARISCHES MUSEUM

Dr. Vernan, 2. Es la más completa colección de vestigios de los habitantes prehispánicos de las Islas Canarias. Interesante sección de antropología, con momias, esqueletos, y cráneos aborígenes, destacando el tipo de Cro Magnon. Colección de cerámica, en la que destacan las «pintadoras», especie de sellos en terracota cuyos dibujos geométricos eran estampados en ocre y rojo sobre la piel y los vestidos de los antiguos canarios. Sección de flora y fauna.

Dr. Vernan, 2. C'est la collection la plus complète de vestiges des habitants préhispaniques des îles Canaries. Une intéressante section d'antropologie, avec des momies, des squelettes et des crânes aborigènes, particulièrement le type de Cro Magnon. Collection de céramiques où sont remarquables les «pintadoras», sorte de sceaux en terre peinte, dont les dessins géometriques étaient imprimés en ocre et en rouge sur la peau et les vètements des anciens canariens. Section de flore et de faune.

Dr. Vernan, 2. This has the fullest collection of the pre-hispanic inhabitants of the Canary Islands. An interesting section of anthropology, with mummies, skeletons and aborigine skulls, with the Cro Magnon type. A ceramics collection, with the famous «pintadoras» a kind of stamp in terracotta with geometric drawings printed in ochre and red on the skin, and the clothes of the ancient Canaries. Flora and Fauna section.

Dr. Vernan, 2. Es beherbergt die vollständigste Sammlung von Uberrresten der prehispanischen inselbewohner. Interessant ist die anthropologische Anteilung mit ihren Mumien, Skeletten und Schädel der Urbewohner, wobei besonders der Typ Cro Magnon hervorzuheben ist. In der Keramikabteilung sind vor allem sehenswert die sog. «pintadoras», Art Terracotta-Stempel, deren geometrische ocker oder rotfarbigen Zeichnungen auf die Leder- und Stoffbekleidung der Urbewohner aufgedruckt wurden Botanische und zoologische Anteilung.

CASA DE COLÓN
MAISON DE COLOMB
HOUSE OF COLUMBUS
HAUS DES KOLUMBUS

Calle de Colón, 1. Antigua residencia de los primeros Gobernadores de la Isla. Posee el doble interés de su belleza arquitectónica y de la colección de objetos y documentos de la época colombina.

Rue de Colón, 1. Ancienne résidence des premiers Gouverneurs de l'Ile. Possède le double intérêt de sa beauté architecturale et de la collection d'objets et documents de l'époque de Colomb.

Calle de Colón, 1. The old residence of the first Governors of the Island. It is interesting for its architectural beauty as welt as for the collection of objects and documents from the Columbian period.

Calle de Colón, 1. Alte Residenz der ersten Gouverneure der Insel. Es ist duppelt interessant wegen seiner architektonischen Schönheil und wegen seiner Sammlung von Gegensfänden und Dokumenten aus der kolumbinischen Zeit.

CASA-MUSEO PÉREZ GALDÓS
MAISON-MUSÉE PÉREZ GALDÓS
PÉREZ GALDÓS HOUSE-MUSEUM
HAUS-MUSEUM PÉREZ GALDÓS

Calle Cano, 33. Se trata de la casa donde nació y vivió el gran novelista español, don Benito Pérez Galdós. Custodia manuscritos, epistolarios, dibujos, etc., y también otros recuerdos personales del ilustre escritor español.

Rue Cano, 33. Il s'agit de la maison où naquit et vécut le grand romancier espagnol, don Benito Pérez Galdós. Elle garde des manuscrits, des épistolaires, des dessins, etc., et aussi d'autres souvenirs personnels de l'illustre écrivain espagnol.

Calle Cano, 33. This is the house where the great Spanish novelist, don Benito Pérez Galdós, was born. It contains manuscripts, letters, drawings, etc., and other personal reminders of the famous Spanish writer.

Rue Cano, 33. Der grosse spanische Romanschriftsteller Benito Pérez Galdós wurde in diesem. Haus geboren und lebte dort. Es zeigt Manuskripte, gesammelte Briefe, Zeichnungen usw. und auch persönliche Dinge aus dem Besitz des berühmten spanischen Schriftstellers.

MUSEO NÉSTOR
MUSÉE NÉSTOR
NÉSTOR MUSEUM
NÉSTOR-MUSEUM

Se halla situado en el Pueblo Canario (Ciudad jardín). En él se exhiben óleos, dibujos, proyectos y, además, numerosos recuerdos personales, del pintor canario Néstor Martín-Fernández de la Torre (1888-1938).

Il se trouve situè dans le Pueblo Canario (Ciudad jardín). On y exhibe des peintures à l'huile, des dessins, des projets et, en outre, de nombreux souvenirs personnels du peintre canarien Néstor Martín-Fernández de la Torre (1888-1938).

It is located in the Canary Island Town (Ciudad jardín). Here are exhibited oil paintings, drawings, plans and many personal reminders of the Canary Island painter Néstor Martín-Fernández de la Torre (1888-1938).

Es befindet sich in dem Kanarischen Dorf (Ciudad jardín-Garfenstadt). Es werden dort Ölgemälde, Zeichnungen, Projekte und ausserdem viele persönliche Gegenstände des kanarischen Malers Néstor Martín-Fernánde de la Torre (1888 bis 1938), gezeigf.

MUSEO DIOCESANO DE ARTE SACRO
MUSÉE DIOCÉSAIN D'ART RELIGIEUX
DIOCESAN MUSEUM OF SACRED ART
DIÖZESANMUSEM DER HEILIGEN KUNST

Consta de seis salas, en las que se exponen magníficas pinturas flamencas y castellanas; esculturas y otros objetos de arte religioso, algunos de los cuales datan del siglo XV. Orfebrería hispano-americana, tapices aztecas y muebles de época. Muchas de estas obras son de gran valor, destacando un Crucifijo atribuido a Alonso Cano, una valiosa colección de imágenes de tallistas canarios de los siglos XVII y XVIII, y un Calvario del escultor canario Luján Pérez.

Formé par six salles où l'on expose de magnifiques peintures flamandes et castillanes; sculptures et d'autres objets d'art religieux, dont certains datent du XVème siècle. Orfèvrerie hispano-américaine, tapis aztèques et mobilier de l'époque. Beaucoup de ces oeuvres sont de grande valeur, et parmi les plus remarquables on y trouve un Crucifix attribué à Alonso Cano, une estimable collection de sculptures des ciseleurs canariens des XVIIème et XVIIIème siècles et un Calvaire du sculpteur canarien Luján Pérez.

Formed by six halls where magnificent Flemish and Castillian paintings can be admired; sculptures and other works of religious art, some of them dating from the XV Century, Spanish-American gold smith works, Aztec tapestry and furniture from that time. Many of these works are of great value, among the most remarkable a Crucifix attributed to Alonso Cano, a valuable collection of images made by Canarian woodcarvers of the XVII and XVIII Centuries, and a Calvary made by the Canarian sculptor Luján Pérez.

Bestehend aus sechs Sälen in den ausgezeichnete flämische und kastilische Gemälde ausgestellt sind; Skulpturen und endere Werke der heiligen Kunst, manche von ihnen aus den XV Jahrhundert stammend, Spanischamerikanische Goldschmiedearbeil, aztekische Teppische und Möbel aus jener Zeit. Viele von diesen Werken sind von grossem Wert, besonders ein Kruzifix welches Alonso Cano zugeschrieben wird, eine kostbare Sammlung von Heiligenbildern kanarischer Künstler aus den XVII und XVIII Jahrhunderten und ein Leidensweg des Kanarischen Bildhauers Luján Pérez.

ARTESANÍA
ARTISANAT
GRAFTWORK
KUNSTHANDWERK

El gusto del pueblo también se manifiesta en su artesanía. Sus bordados y cerámicas son resultado de una vieja tradición que se conserva en muchos pueblos del interior. Se fabrican también cestos de hoja de palma, tejidos de lana y de lino, objetos fallados en madera y cuchillos canarios de empuñadura finamente labrada. Actualmente la manufactura de cigarros, que ha conseguido una alta reputación internacional, es la más reciente expresión de la maestría artesana del isleño.

Le goût populaire se manifeste aussi dans l'artisanat. Les broderies et les céramiques sont le fruit d'une vieille tradition conservée dans beaucoup de villages de l'intérieur. On fabrique aussi des paniers avec des feuilles de palmier, des tissus de laine et de lin, des objets taillés dans le bois et des couteaux canariens au manche finement ouvré. La fabrication des cigares et cigarettes, qui est la plus récente manifestacion de la maîtrise artisanale insulaire, a attcint une haute réputation internationale.

Their embroidery qnd ceramics have inherited an age-old tradition that has survived in many inland villages. Other products of their craftsmanship include palm-leaf baskets, wool and linen materials, wood-carvings and Canary-Island knives with intricately designed hilts. The latest illustration of the islanders' skills is the production of cigars that have wan high reputations throughout the world.

Der Geschmack des Volkes kommf auch in seinem Handwerk zum Ausdruck. Seine Stickereien und Keramikarbeiten sind das Ergebnis einer alten Tradition, die sich in vielen Dörfern des Inneren erhalten hat. Es werden auch aus Palmblättern Körbe hergestellt, Stoffe aus Wolle und Leinen, holzgeschnitzte Gegenstände und kanarische Messer mit fein ausgeführtem Griff. Gegenwärtig ist die Zigarettenfabrikation, die einen hohen internationalen Ruf eelangt hat, der jüngste Ausdruck der handwerklichen Fertigkeit der Inselbewohner.

127

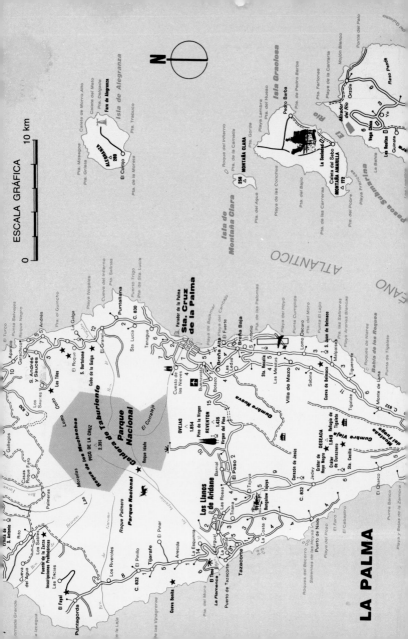